Human Resource Management

Essential Perspectives

fourth edition

Robert L. Mathis
University of Nebraska at Omaha

John H. Jackson
University of Wyoming

THOMSON
™
SOUTH-WESTERN

Australia • Brazil • Canada • Mexico • Singapore • Spain • United Kingdom • United States

THOMSON

SOUTH-WESTERN

Human Resource Management: Essential Perspectives, Fourth Edition
Robert L. Mathis and John H. Jackson

VP/Editorial Director:
Jack W. Calhoun

Editor-in-Chief:
Melissa S. Acuña

Senior Acquisitions Editor:
Joe Sabatino

Senior Developmental Editor:
Mardell Glinski Schultz

Senior Marketing Manager:
Kimberly Kanakes

Production Project Manager:
Margaret M. Bril

Manager of Technology, Editorial:
Vicky True

Technology Project Editor:
Kristen Meere

Web Coordinator:
Karen Schaffer

Senior Manufacturing Coordinator:
Diane Lohman

Production House:
International Typesetting and Composition

Printer:
Transcontinental
Louiseville, QC J5V 1B4

Art Director:
Linda Helcher

Internal Designer:
Grannan Graphic Design, Ltd.

Cover Designer:
Grannan Graphic Design, Ltd.

Library of Congress Control Number:
2005937605

For more information about our products, contact us at:

Thomson Learning Academic Resource Center

1-800-423-0563

Thomson Higher Education
5191 Natorp Boulevard
Mason, OH 45040
USA

About the Authors

DR. ROBERT L. MATHIS

Dr. Robert Mathis is a Professor of Management at the University of Nebraska at Omaha (UNO). Born and raised in Texas, he received a BBA and MBA from Texas Tech University and a Ph.D. in management and organization from the University of Colorado. At UNO he received the university's "Excellence in Teaching" award.

Dr. Mathis has co-authored several books and published numerous articles covering a variety of topics over the last twenty-five years. On the professional level, Dr. Mathis has held numerous national offices in the Society for Human Resource Management and in other professional organizations, including the Academy of Management. He also served as President of the Human Resource Certification Institute (HRCI) and is certified as a Senior Professional in Human Resources (SPHR) by HRCI.

He has had extensive consulting experiences with organizations of all sizes in a variety of areas. Firms assisted have been in telecommunications, telemarketing, financial, manufacturing, retail, health care, and utility industries. He has extensive specialized consulting experience in establishing or revising compensation plans for small and medium-sized firms. Internationally, Dr. Mathis has consulting and training experience with organizations in Australia, Lithuania, Romania, Moldova, and Taiwan.

DR. JOHN H. JACKSON

Dr. John H. Jackson is a Professor of Management at the University of Wyoming. Born in Alaska, he received his BBA and MBA from Texas Tech University. He then worked in the telecommunications industry in human resources management for several years. After leaving that industry, he completed his doctoral studies at the University of Colorado and received his Ph.D. in management and organization.

During his academic career, Dr. Jackson has authored six other college texts and more than fifty articles and papers, including those appearing in *Academy of Management Review, Journal of Management, Human Resources Management,* and *Human Resource Planning.* He has consulted with a variety of organizations on HR and management development matters and served as an expert witness in a number of HR-related cases.

At the University of Wyoming he served three terms as department head in the Department of Management and Marketing. Dr. Jackson received the university's highest teaching award and worked with two-way interactive television for MBA students. He designed one of the first classes in the nation on Business, Environment, and Natural Resources. Two Wyoming state governors have appointed him to the Wyoming Business Council and the Workforce Development Council. Dr. Jackson is also president of Silverwood Ranches, Inc.

Preface

The importance of human resource issues for managers and organizations is evident every day. As indicated by frequent headlines and news media reports on downsizing, workforce shortages, sexual harassment, union activity, and other topics, the management of human resources is growing in importance in the United States and the world. Many individuals are affected by HR issues; consequently, they will benefit by becoming more knowledgeable about HR management. Those interested in the field of HR management must understand more about the nature of various HR activities. Every manager's HR actions can have major consequences for organizations. This book has been prepared to provide an essential overview of HR management for students, HR practitioners, and others in organizations.

A need exists for an overview of HR management that both HR practitioners and students can use. The positive reception of the previous editions of *Human Resource Management: Essential Perspectives* proved this need. Consequently, we are pleased to provide an updated version. In addition, this book presents information in a way that is useful to various industry groups and professional organizations. Finally, this condensed view of HR management also addresses the tremendous interest in U.S. practices of HR management in other countries, making it a valuable resource for managers worldwide.

As authors, it is our belief that this book will be a useful and interesting resource for those desiring a concise discussion of the important issues and practices in HR management. It is our hope that it will contribute to more effective management of human resources in organizations.

Robert L. Mathis, Ph.D., SPHR
John H. Jackson, Ph.D.

Table of Contents

Chapter 1

Changing Nature of Human Resource Management

For many organizations, talented employees are the cornerstone of a competitive advantage. If the organization competes based on new ideas, outstanding customer service, or quick, accurate decisions, having excellent employees is critical. Of course, not every organization must compete on the basis of having the best employees, but even for those that do not, employees are a major source of performance, problems, growth, resistance, and lawsuits.

1. Why must HR management transform from being primarily administrative and operational to become a more strategic contributor?

2. Describe how economic and workforce changes are affecting organizations in which you have worked, and give specific examples of how these changes should be addressed.

3. What steps can HR professionals take to overcome the view that what HR accomplishes is not measurable?

NATURE OF HUMAN RESOURCE MANAGEMENT

As a field, human resource (HR) management is undergoing significant transformation. **Human Resource management** is the direction of organizational systems to ensure that human talent is used effectively and efficiently to accomplish organizational goals. Whether employees are in a big company with 10,000 positions or a small nonprofit agency with 10 positions, these employees must be recruited, selected, trained, and managed. They also must be compensated, and many will be given benefits of some type, which means that an appropriate and legal compensation system is needed. In an environment in which the workforce keeps changing, laws and the needs of employers change too.[1] Therefore, HR management activities continue to change and evolve.

HR Activities

HR management is composed of seven interlinked activities taking place within organizations, as depicted in Figure 1.1. Additionally, external forces—legal, economic, technological, global, environmental, cultural/geographic, political,

FIGURE 1.1   HR Management Activities

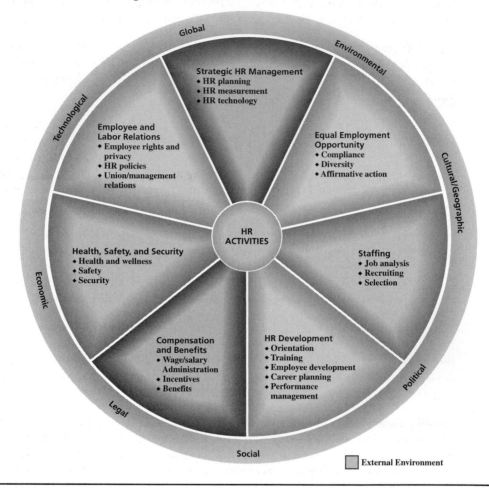

and social—significantly affect HR activities and how they are designed, managed, and changed.

Global Forces and HR Management HR management truly is becoming transnational as organizations compete globally. For instance, in the past few years, the international outsourcing of U.S. jobs to India, the Philippines, China, and other countries has become a significant political concern. Also, the worldwide growth of global firms such as Toyota and SAP means that management must consider transnational concerns in all HR activities.

Strategic HR Management To anticipate and respond to the HR changes facing organizations, strategic HR management has grown in importance. As part of maintaining organizational competitiveness, *HR effectiveness* must be increased through the use of *HR metrics*. One key to increasing HR effectiveness is using *HR technology.* Many organizations have *HR management systems (HRMSs)*, which use information technology to provide managers and employees with more accurate and timely information on HR programs and activities.

Equal Employment Opportunity *Compliance* with equal employment opportunity (EEO) laws and regulations affects all other HR activities and is integral to HR management. The *diversity* of a multicultural and global workforce is creating more challenges for HR professionals and all managers.

Staffing The aim of staffing is to provide an adequate supply of qualified individuals to fill jobs in an organization. By studying what workers do, *job analysis* lays the foundation for the staffing function. Then both *job descriptions* and *job specifications* can be prepared to use when *recruiting* applicants for job openings. The *selection* process is concerned with choosing qualified individuals to fill jobs in the organization.

HR Development Beginning with the *orientation* of new employees, HR development includes different types of *job-skill training.* Also, *development* of all employees, including supervisors and managers, is necessary to prepare organizations for future challenges. *Career planning* identifies paths and activities for individual employees as they develop within the organization. Assessing how employees perform their jobs is the focus of *performance management.*

Compensation and Benefits Compensation in the form of *pay, incentives,* and *benefits* rewards people for performing organizational work. Employers must develop and refine their basic *wage and salary* systems. Also, the use of *incentive programs* such as gainsharing and productivity rewards is growing.

Health, Safety, and Security Ensuring the physical and mental health and safety of employees is vital. The Occupational Safety and Health Act (OSHA) of 1970 has made organizations more responsive to concerns for *safety* through a focus on reducing work-related illnesses, accidents, and injuries. Through a broader focus on *health,* HR management can use *employee assistance programs (EAPs)* to help employees with substance abuse and other problems and thereby retain otherwise satisfactory employees.

Employee and Labor Relations The relationship between managers and their employees must be handled effectively if both the employees and the organization are to prosper together. Whether or not some of the employees are represented by a union, *employee rights* must be addressed. It is important to develop, communicate, and update HR *policies and procedures* so that managers and employees alike know what is expected. In some organizations, *union/management relations* must be addressed as well.

HR in Organizations

In a real sense, *every* manager in an organization is an HR manager. Sales managers, head nurses, drafting supervisors, college deans, and accounting supervisors all engage in HR management, and their effectiveness depends in part on the success of organizational HR systems. However, it is unrealistic to expect a nursing supervisor or an engineering manager to know about the nuances of equal employment regulations, or how to design and administer a compensation and benefits system. For this reason, larger organizations frequently have people in an HR department who specialize in these activities.

Human Capital and HR

Human capital is not the people in organizations—it is what those people bring and contribute to organizational success.[2] **Human capital** is the collective value of the capabilities, knowledge, skills, life experiences, and motivation of an organizational workforce.

Sometimes it is called *intellectual capital* to reflect the thinking, knowledge, creativity, and decision making that people in organizations contribute. For example, firms with high intellectual capital may have technical and research employees who create new biomedical devices, formulate pharmaceuticals that can be patented, and develop new software for specialized uses. All these organizational contributions indicate the value of human capital.

Human Resources as a Core Competency

The development and implementation of specific organizational strategies must be based on the areas of strength in an organization. Referred to as *core competencies,* these strengths are the foundation for creating a competitive advantage for an organization. A **core competency** is a unique capability that creates high value and differentiates an organization from its competition.

HR MANAGEMENT CHALLENGES

The environment faced by organizations and their managers is a challenging one. A force affecting the management of human resources is the *globalization of business,* as shown in such areas as international outsourcing and global competitive pressures.

Globalization of Business

It has been estimated that during the past few years almost 600,000 U.S. jobs have been "transferred" to foreign locations. The primary reason for these shifts is to save on labor costs.[3]

Economic and Technological Changes

Economic and technological changes have altered several occupational and employment patterns in the United States. Several of these changes are discussed next.

Occupational Shifts A major change is the shift of jobs from manufacturing and agriculture to service and telecommunications. In general, the U.S. economy has become predominately a service economy, and that shift is expected to continue. Over 80% of U.S. jobs are in service industries, and most new jobs created by the year 2010 will also be in services.[4]

Workforce Availability and Quality Concerns Many parts of the United States face significant workforce shortages that exist due to an inadequate supply of workers with the skills needed to perform the jobs being added. It is not that there are too few people—only that there are too few with the skills being demanded. For instance, a study of U.S. manufacturing firms revealed that about 80% of them have been experiencing a moderate to serious shortage of qualified workers. The primary reasons were shifting demographics, the negative image of the manufacturing industry, and inadequately educated U.S. workers.[5]

Growth in Contingent Workforce "Contingent workers" (temporary workers, independent contractors, leased employees, and part-timers) represent more than 20% of the U.S. workforce. The use of contingent workers has grown for many reasons. A significant one is that many contingent workers are paid less and/or receive fewer benefits than regular employees. Omitting contingent workers from health-care benefits saves some firms 20% to 40% in labor costs.

Technological Shifts and the Internet Globalization and economic shifts have been accelerated by technological changes, with the Internet being a primary driver. The explosive growth in information technology and in the use of the Internet has driven changes in jobs and organizations of all sizes.

Workforce Demographics and Diversity

The U.S. workforce has been changing dramatically. It is more diverse racially and ethnically, more women are in it than ever before, and the average age of its members is now considerably older. As a result of these demographic shifts, HR management in organizations has had to adapt to a more varied labor force both externally and internally.

Racial/Ethnic Diversity Racial and ethnic minorities account for a growing percentage of the overall labor force, with the percentage of Hispanics equal to or greater than the percentage of African Americans. Immigrants will continue to expand this growth. An increasing number of individuals characterize themselves as *multiracial,* suggesting that the American "melting pot" is blurring racial and ethnic identities.

Women in the Workforce Women constitute about 47% of the workforce in the United States and 43% in Europe.[6] Many women workers are single, separated, divorced, or widowed, and therefore are "primary" income earners. Many women who are married have spouses who are also employed. A growing number of households in the United States include "domestic partners," who are committed to each other though not married and who may be of the same or the opposite sex.

Aging Workforce In many economically developed countries, the population is aging, resulting in a significantly aging workforce. In the United States, over the next decade, a significant number of experienced employees will be retiring, changing to part-time, or otherwise shifting their employment. Replacing the experience and talents of longer-service workers is a growing challenge facing employers in all industries.

HR MANAGEMENT ROLES

Several roles can be fulfilled by HR management. The nature and extent of these roles depends on both what upper management wants HR management to do and what competencies the HR staff have demonstrated. Three roles are typically identified for HR:

▶ *Administrative:* Focusing on HR clerical administration and recordkeeping
▶ *Operational and employee advocate:* Managing most HR activities and serving as employee "champion"
▶ *Strategic:* Becoming a contributor to organizational results and the "keeper" of organizational ethics

The administrative role has been the dominant part of HR. However, as Figure 1.2 indicates, a significant transformation in HR is occurring. The HR

FIGURE 1.2   Changing Roles of HR Management

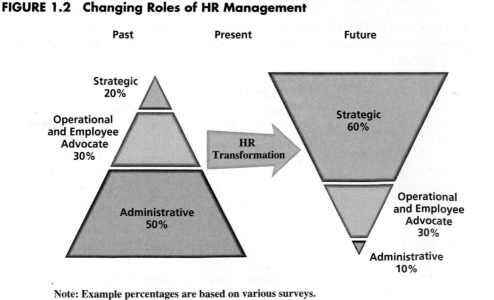

Note: Example percentages are based on various surveys.

pyramid is having to be turned upside down, so that significantly less HR time and fewer HR staff are used for clerical administration.

Administrative Role of HR

The administrative role of HR management has been heavily oriented to processing and record keeping. If limited to the administrative role, HR staff is seen primarily as clerical and lower-level administrative contributors to the organization.

Two major shifts driving the transformation of the administrative role are greater use of technology and outsourcing. According to various surveys by outsourcing firms, the areas most commonly outsourced are employee assistance/counseling, pension/retirement planning, benefits administration, training, and payroll services.[7] The primary reasons why HR functions are outsourced is to save money on HR staffing, to take advantage of specialized vendor expertise and technology, and to be able to focus on more strategic HR activities.

Operational and Employee Advocate Role for HR

Traditionally, HR has been viewed as the "employee advocate" in organizations. As the voice for employee concerns, someone must be the "champion" for employees and employee issues.

The operational role requires HR professionals to identify and implement needed programs and policies in the organization, in cooperation with operating managers. This role traditionally includes many of the HR activities mentioned earlier in the chapter.

Strategic Role for HR

Differences between the operational and strategic approaches in a number of HR areas exist. The strategic HR role requires that HR professionals be proactive in addressing business realities and focus on future HR needs, such as workforce planning, compensation strategies, and demonstrating the value of HR to top management.

Many executives, managers, and HR professionals increasingly see the need for HR management to become a greater strategic contributor to the "business" success of organizations. Even organizations that are not-for-profit, such as governmental and social service entities, must manage their human resources in a "business-oriented" manner.

The role of HR as a *strategic business partner* is often described as "having a seat at the table," and contributing to the strategic directions and success of the organization. This role means partnering with the chief financial officers (CFOs) and meeting the expectations of the chief executive officers (CEOs).

HR TECHNOLOGY

The use of information technology of all types is transforming the various roles of HR management. Greater use of technology has led to organizational use of a **human resource management system (HRMS),** which is an integrated system providing information used by HR management in decision making. The HRMS terminology emphasizes that making HR decisions, not just building databases, is the primary reason for compiling data in an information system.

ETHICS AND HR MANAGEMENT

Closely linked with the strategic role of HR is the way HR management professionals influence the organizational ethics practiced by executives, managers, and employees. On the strategic level, organizations with high ethical standards are more likely to meet long-term strategic objectives and profit goals. Organizations that are seen as operating with integrity are viewed more positively by individuals in the community and in the industry, as well as by consumers and employees. This positive view often translates into bottom-line financial results and the ability to attract and retain human resources.

HR plays a key role in ensuring ethical behavior in organizations because the number of employees reporting ethical misconduct has grown in the past few years, primarily because of the corporate scandals from several years earlier. When the following four elements of ethics programs exist, ethical behavior is likely to occur:

▶ A written code of ethics and standards of conduct
▶ Training on ethical behavior for all executives, managers, and employees
▶ Means for employees to obtain advice on ethical situations they face, often provided by HR
▶ Systems for confidential reporting of ethical misconduct or questionable behavior

HR Management as a Career Field

There are a variety of jobs within the HR career field, ranging from executive to clerical. As an employer grows large enough to need someone to focus primarily on HR activities, the role of the **HR generalist** emerges—that is, a person who is responsible for performing a variety of HR activities. Further growth leads to the addition of **HR specialists,** or individuals who have in-depth knowledge and expertise in limited areas of HR.

NATURE OF STRATEGIC HR MANAGEMENT

Strategic HR management refers to the use of employees to gain or keep a competitive advantage, resulting in greater organizational effectiveness. Figure 1.3 shows the factors that affect strategic HR management.

There should be a close relationship between organizational strategy and HR strategy. Two basic types of organizational strategies can be identified: *cost-leadership* and *differentiation.* A company like Wal-Mart follows a cost-leadership strategy, and firms like Intel or Microsoft follow a differentiation strategy. A cost-leadership

FIGURE 1.3   Strategic HR Management Process

strategy approaches competition on the basis of low price and high quality of product or service. The differentiation strategy is more appropriate in a more dynamic environment characterized by rapid change, and requires continually finding new products and new markets. The two strategies may not be mutually exclusive; it is possible for an organization to pursue one strategy with some products or services, and the other strategy with other products or services.

Every organization has a mission that identifies its reasons for existence. To fulfill its mission, the organization must have goals and objectives to achieve. For example, a hospital exists to provide health-care services. To meet its mission, the hospital must set specific targets and state desired results. One target that the hospital may wish to meet is an 80% average occupancy rate (that is, 400 of its 500 beds occupied on the average day) so that it receives enough income to pay for its building debt, equipment, employees, and other expenses.

HR management plays a significant strategic role. In organizations where there are identifiable HR "strengths," organizational effectiveness is enhanced. Strategic HR management plays a significant role in several dimensions of organizational effectiveness. Four prominent ones are as follows:

► Organizational productivity
► Financial contributions
► Service and quality
► Organizational culture

Organizational Productivity and HR Efforts

A useful way of measuring HR productivity of human resources is to consider **unit labor cost,** which is computed by dividing the average cost of workers by their average levels of output. Using unit labor costs, one can see that paying relatively high wages still can result in a firm being economically competitive if high productivity levels are achieved. Low unit labor costs can be a basis for a strategy focusing on human resources. Productivity and unit labor costs can be evaluated at the global, country, organizational, or individual level.

Organizational Effectiveness and Financial Contributions of HR

A second aspect of organizational effectiveness relates to HR management being a financial contributor. During the past several years, HR management has given significant attention to linking more effectively with financial executives, including Chief Financial Officers (CFOs). The purpose of this linkage has been to make certain that HR is a financial contributor to organizational effectiveness.

Customer Service and Quality Linked to HR Strategies

In addition to productivity, customer service and quality significantly affect organizational effectiveness. Having all employees focus on customers contributes significantly to achieving organizational goals and maintaining a competitive advantage. In many organizations, service quality is greatly influenced by the individual employees who interact with customers. For instance, organizations with high turnover rates of employees quitting their jobs have seen slow sales growth. It seems customers see continuity of customer service representatives as important in making sales decisions. Unfortunately, overall customer satisfaction with sales quality has declined in the United States and other countries.[8]

Organizational Culture and Organizational Effectiveness

The shared values and beliefs in an organization is the **organizational culture.** Managers definitely must consider the culture of the organization, because otherwise excellent strategies can be negated by a culture incompatible with those strategies. Further, the culture of the organization, as viewed by the people in it, affects attraction and retention of competent employees.

HUMAN RESOURCE PLANNING

The competitive strategies and objectives of an organization are the foundation for **human resource (HR) planning,** which is the process of analyzing and identifying the need for and availability of human resources so that the organization can meet its objectives. HR plans must be "linked" effectively with strategic plans for human resources to be a "core competency" that provides competitive advantage for the organization. For instance, both FedEx and UPS have identified their human resources as being key to achieving their organizational strategic goals. Even though they are competitors, both firms have emphasized HR efforts as key to organizational success. However, the unique nature of each organization and its culture has led to differing HR strategies and plans.

The focus of HR planning is to have the *right number of human resources,* with the *right capabilities,* at the *right times,* and in the *right places.* In HR planning, an organization must consider the availability of and allocation of people to jobs over long periods of time, not just for the next month or even the next year. Therefore, HR planning at Walgreen's has had to identify how and where to find enough pharmacists to fill openings caused by turnover and retirement, as well as to staff all the new stores.[9]

HR Planning Process

The steps in the HR planning process are shown in Figure 1.4. Notice that the HR planning process begins with considering the organizational objectives and strategies. Then HR needs and supply sources must be analyzed both externally

FIGURE 1.4   HR Planning Process

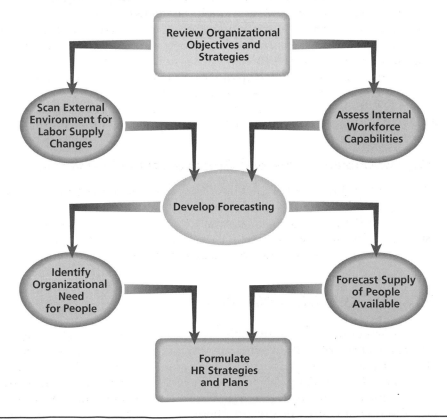

and internally, and forecasts must be developed. Key to assessing internal human resources is having solid information accessible through a human resource management system (HRMS).

Once the assessments are complete, forecasts must be developed to identify the relationship between supply and demand for human resources. Management then formulates HR strategies and plans to address imbalances, both short term and long term.

HR strategies are means used to anticipate and manage the supply of and demand for human resources. These strategies provide overall direction for the ways HR activities will be designed and managed. Finally, specific HR plans are developed to provide more specific direction for the management of HR activities. The most telling evidence of successful HR planning is a consistent alignment of the availabilities and capabilities of human resources with the needs of the organization over a period of time.

SCANNING THE EXTERNAL ENVIRONMENT

At the heart of strategic planning is environmental scanning, a process of studying the environment of the organization to pinpoint opportunities and threats. The external environment especially affects HR planning because each organization must draw from the same labor market that supplies all other employers. Indeed, one measure of organizational effectiveness is the ability of an organization to compete for a sufficient supply of human resources with the appropriate capabilities. All elements of the external environment—government influences, economic conditions, geographic and competition issues, and workforce changes—must be part of the scanning process.

ASSESSING THE INTERNAL WORKFORCE

Analyzing the jobs that will need to be done and the skills of people who are currently available in the organization to do them is the next part of HR planning. The needs of the organization must be compared against the labor supply available inside the organization.

Jobs and Skills Audit

The starting point for evaluating internal strengths and weaknesses is an audit of the jobs being done in the organization. The following questions are addressed during the internal assessment:

▶ What jobs exist now?
▶ How many individuals are performing each job?
▶ What are the reporting relationships of jobs?
▶ How essential is each job?
▶ What jobs will be needed to implement future organizational strategies?
▶ What are the characteristics of anticipated jobs?

Organizational Capabilities Inventory

As HR planners gain an understanding of the current and future jobs that will be necessary to carry out organizational plans, they can make a detailed audit of current employees and their capabilities. The basic source of data on employees is the HR records in the organization. Different HR information databases can be used to identify the knowledge, skills, and abilities (KSAs) of employees. Planners can use KSA inventories to determine future needs for recruiting, selection, and HR development. The information in these inventories can also provide a basis for determining what additional capabilities will be needed in the future workforce.

FORECASTING HR SUPPLY AND DEMAND

The information gathered from scanning the external environmental and assessing internal strengths and weaknesses is used to predict HR supply and demand in light of organizational objectives and strategies. **Forecasting** uses information from the past and the present to identify expected future conditions. Projections for the future are, of course, subject to error. Usually, though, experienced people are able to forecast with enough accuracy to benefit long-range organizational planning.

HR forecasting should be done over three planning periods: short range, intermediate-range, and long-range. The most commonly used planning period of six months to one year focuses on *short-range* forecasts for the immediate HR needs of an organization. Intermediate- and long-range forecasting are much more difficult processes. *Intermediate-range* plans usually project one to five years into the future, and *long-range* plans extend beyond five years.

Forecasting the Demand for Human Resources

The demand for employees can be calculated for an entire organization and/or for individual units in the organization. Demand for human resources can be forecast by considering specific openings that are likely to occur. The openings (or demands) are created when employees leave positions because of promotions, transfers, and terminations. The analysis always begins with the top positions in the organization, because from there, no promotions to a higher level are possible.

Forecasting the Supply of Human Resources

Once human resources needs have been forecast, then availability of human resources must be identified. Forecasting the availability considers both *external* and *internal* supplies. Although the internal supply may be easier to calculate, it is important to calculate the external supply as accurately as possible.

External Supply The external supply of potential employees available to the organization needs to be identified. Extensive use of government estimates of labor force populations, trends in the industry, and many more complex and

FIGURE 1.5 Estimating Internal Labor Supply for a Given Unit

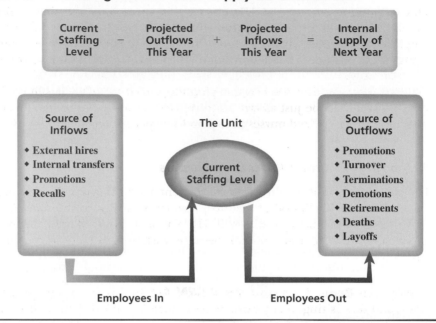

interrelated factors must be considered. Such information is often available from state or regional economic development offices, including these:

▶ Net migration into and out of the area
▶ Individuals entering and leaving the workforce
▶ Individuals graduating from schools and colleges
▶ Changing workforce composition and patterns
▶ Economic forecasts for the next few years
▶ Technological developments and shifts
▶ Actions of competing employers
▶ Government regulations and pressures
▶ Circumstances affecting persons entering and leaving the workforce

Internal Supply Figure 1.5 shows in general terms how the internal supply can be calculated for a specific employer. Estimating internal supply considers that employees move from their current jobs into others through promotions, lateral moves, and terminations. It also considers that the internal supply is influenced by training and development programs, transfer and promotion policies, and retirement policies, among other factors. In forecasting the internal supply, data from the replacement charts and succession planning efforts are used to project potential personnel changes, identify possible backup candidates, and keep track of attrition (resignations, retirements, etc.) for each department in an organization.

Succession Planning

One important outcome of HR planning is **succession planning,** which is a process of identifying a longer-term plan for the orderly replacement of key employees. In larger organizations, such as the U.S. federal government, the aging of the workforce has significant implications for HR planning and succession planning.

One common flaw in succession planning is that too often it is limited to key executives. It may be just as critical to replace several experienced mechanical engineers or specialized nurses as to plan for replacing the CEO.

Managing a Human Resources Surplus

HR planning is of little value if no subsequent action is taken. The action taken depends on the likelihood of a human resources surplus or shortage. A surplus of workers can be managed within an HR plan in a variety of ways. Regardless of the means, the actions are difficult because workforce reductions are ultimately necessary.

Workforce Reductions and the WARN Act In this era of mergers, acquisitions, and downsizing, many workers have been laid off or had their jobs eliminated due to the closing of selected offices, plants, and operations. To provide employees with sufficient notice of such losses, a federal law passed the Worker Adjustment and Retraining Notification (WARN) Act. This law requires employers to give a 60-day notice before implementing a layoff or facility closing that involves more than 50 people.

HR Planning in Mergers and Acquisitions

Another HR concern has been the proliferation of mergers and acquisitions in many industries. One has only to look at the financial or telecommunications industry to see massive consolidation in the number of firms. A common result of most mergers and acquisitions (M&As) is an excess of employees once the firms have been combined, due to redundant departments, plants, and people. Because much of the rationale for combinations is financial, eliminating employees with overlapping responsibilities is a primary concern.

MEASURING HR EFFECTIVENESS USING HR METRICS

During the past several years, the importance of measuring HR effectiveness has grown. A number of writers have stressed that HR cannot be a strategic business contributor without focusing on measuring its programs, its services, and its contributions to organizational success. It is through the development and use of metrics that HR can better demonstrate its value and track its performance.

HR metrics are specific measures tied to HR performance indicators. A metric can be developed using costs, quantity, quality, timeliness, and other designated goals. One pioneer in developing HR measurements, Jac Fitz-Enz, has identified a wide range of HR metrics.[10]

Measures of Strategic HR Effectiveness

For HR to fulfill its role as a strategic business partner, HR metrics that reflect organizational strategies and goods must be used. Some of the more prevalent measures compare *full-time equivalents* (FTEs) with organizational measures. An FTE is a measure equal to one person working full-time for a year. For instance, two employees each working half-time would count as one FTE.

Return on Investment A widely used financial measure that can be applied to measure the contribution and cost of HR activities is **return on investment (ROI),** which is a calculation showing the value of expenditures for HR activities. It can also be used to show how long it will take for the activities to pay for themselves.

Economic Value Added Another measure used is **economic value added (EVA),** which is the net operating profit of a firm after the cost of capital is deducted. Cost of capital is the minimum rate of return demanded by shareholders. When a company is making more than the cost of capital, it is creating wealth for shareholders. An EVA approach requires that all policies, procedures, measures, and methods use cost of capital as a benchmark against which their return is judged. Human resource decisions can be subjected to the same analyses.

HR and the Balanced Scorecard One effective approach to the measurement of the strategic performance of organizations, including their HR departments, is the *balanced scorecard.* Use of the balanced scorecard stresses measuring the strategic performance of organizations on four perspectives [11]

- ▶ Financial
- ▶ Internal business processes
- ▶ Customer
- ▶ Learning and growth

HR Measurement and Benchmarking

One approach to assessing HR effectiveness is **benchmarking,** which compares specific measures of performance against data on those measures in other organizations. HR professionals interested in benchmarking compare their measurement data with those from outside sources, including individual companies, industry sources, and professional associations.

Some diagnostic measures can be used to check the effectiveness of the HR function. For benchmarking overall HR costs, one useful source is data gathered each year by SHRM and the Bureau of National Affairs. This survey shows that HR expenditures by workforce size vary significantly. As might be expected, the total number of staff needed to serve 1,000 employees is not significantly different from the number needed to serve 2,500 employees. But the cost per employee of having an HR department is greater in organizations with fewer than 250 employees.

HR Audit

One general means for assessing HR is through an **HR audit** which is a formal research effort that evaluates the current state of HR management in an organization. This audit attempts to evaluate how well HR activities in each of the HR areas (staffing, compensation, health and safety, etc.) have been performed, so that management can identify areas for improvement.

Regardless of the time and effort placed on HR measurement and HR metrics, the most important consideration is that HR effectiveness and efficiency must be measured regularly for HR staff and other managers to know how HR is contributing to organizational success.

NOTES

1. *Small Business by the Numbers* and other reports from the U.S. Small Business Administration, *http://www.sba.gov.*

2. For a useful overview of human capital, see L. A. Weatherly, "Human Capital—The Elusive Asset," *SHRM Research Quarterly*, March 2003.

3. Adapted from data at Forrester Research (*http://www.forrester.com*); Stephanie Armour and Michelle Kessler, "USA's New Money-Saving Export: White Collar Jobs," *USA Today*, August 5, 2003, 1B; Pete Engardio, Aaron Bernstein, and Manjeet Kripalani, "Is Your Job Next?" *Business Week*, February 2003, 50–60; and Maureen Minehan, "Offshore Outsourcing Stirs Controversy," *Global Perspectives*, July 2003.

4. U.S. Bureau of Labor Statistics, 2004, *http://www.bls.gov.*

5. *Keeping America Competitive: How a Talent Shortage Threatens U.S. Manufacturing* (Washington, DC: National Association of Manufacturers, 2003).

6. "Europe Looking to Women for Declining Work Force," *Omaha World-Herald*, December 22, 2003, D1.

7. "Internal HR: Outsourcing Growth," *Workforce Management*, December 2003, 89; and Beth McConnell, "Small Majority of Companies Outsource Some HR Duties," *HR News*, August 14, 2003, *http://www.shrm. org/hrnews.*

8. Regular updates on customer satisfaction generally and by industry are available at *http://www.theacsi.org.*

9. Jeff Barbian, "Medicine for Managers," *Training*, February 2002, 22.

10. How to measure HR activities by areas is described in detail in Jac Fitz-Enz and Barbara Davidson, *How to Measure Human Resources* (New York: McGraw-Hill, 2002).

11. Robert S. Kaplan and David P. Norton, *The Strategy-Focused Organization: How Balanced Scorecard Companies Thrive in the New Business Environment* (Boston: Harvard Business School Press, 2001).

INTERNET RESOURCES

Saratoga Institute This organization is well-known for its HR benchmarking data and studies. **http://www.saratogainstitute.com**

Society for Human Resource Management SHRM is the largest association devoted to Human Resource Management, and this site contains extensive resources. **http://www.shrm.org**

SUGGESTED READINGS

Ralph Christensen, *Roadmap to Strategic HR,* (New York: AMACOM, 2005).

Dennis J. Kravetz, *Measuring Human Capital,* (Mesa, AZ: Kravetz Associates, 2004).

Jack J. Phillips, *Investing in Your Company's Human Capital,* (New York: AMACOM, 2005).

Dave Ulrich, et al., *The Future of Human Resource Management,* (Alexandria, VA: SHRM/ John Wiley & Sons, 2005).

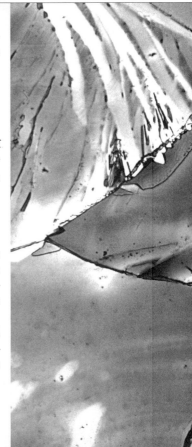

Chapter 2

Organization/Individual Relations and Retention

Relationships between individuals and their employing organizations can vary widely. Both parties may view the employer/employee relationship as satisfactory. Or one may see it as satisfactory and one may not. Or both may be looking for a way to end the relationship. *Job satisfaction* and *commitment* often help determine whether an employee will want to stay. The *individual's performance* is a major part of whether the employer wants the employee to stay. However, understanding the relationship between individuals and organizations is critical for dealing successfully with absenteeism and turnover, a key to understanding individual performance, and vital to retaining employees.

Managerial Perspectives on HR

1. Why has employee retention become a growing concern for many employers?
2. What actions would you suggest to reduce employee absenteeism and turnover?
3. How are the changes occurring in jobs in many organizations affecting HR management?

INDIVIDUAL/ORGANIZATIONAL RELATIONSHIPS

The long-term economic health of most organizations depends on the efforts of employees with both the appropriate capabilities and the motivation to do their jobs well. Organizations that are successful over time can usually demonstrate that relationships with their employees *do* matter.

The Psychological Contract

One concept that has been useful in discussing employees' relationships with organizations is that of a **psychological contract,** which refers to the unwritten expectations employees and employers have about the nature of their work relationships. Because the psychological contract is individual and subjective, it focuses on expectations about "fairness" that may not be defined clearly by employees.

Both tangible items (such as wages, benefits, employee productivity, and attendance) and intangible items (such as loyalty, fair treatment, and job security) are encompassed by unwritten psychological contracts between employers and employees. In a psychological contract:

Employers Provide:	**Employees Contribute:**
▶ Competitive compensation and benefits	▶ Continuous skill improvement and increased productivity
▶ Career development opportunities	▶ Reasonable time with the organization
▶ Flexibility to balance work and home life	▶ Extra effort when needed

Recent research suggests that psychological contracts can be strengthened and employee commitment enhanced when the organization is involved in a cause the employee values highly. Conversely, psychological contracts can be violated not only in reaction to personal mistreatment, but from a perception that the organization has abandoned an important principle or cause.[1]

It is important here to emphasize that people's expectations about psychological contracts differ between generations, as well as within generations. For employers, the differing expectations present challenges. For instance, many baby boomers and matures are concerned about security and experience. However, younger generation Yers are often seen as the "why" generation, who expect to be rewarded quickly, are very adaptable, and tend to ask more questions about why managers and organizations make the decisions they do.

Job Satisfaction, Loyalty, and Commitment

In its most basic sense, **job satisfaction** is a positive emotional state resulting from evaluating one's job experiences. *Job dissatisfaction* occurs when one's expectations are not met. For example, if an employee expects clean and safe working conditions, then the employee is likely to be dissatisfied if the workplace is dirty and dangerous.

Dimensions of job satisfaction frequently mentioned include work, pay, promotion opportunities, supervision, and coworkers. Job satisfaction appears to have declined somewhat in recent years, and elements of the employee/employer relationship were cited among the major reasons in one study.[2] More demanding work, fewer traditional hierarchical relationships with management, shorter relationships, and less confidence in long-term rewards were the reasons cited most frequently.

Loyalty and Organizational Commitment

Even though job satisfaction itself is important, perhaps the "bottom line" is how job satisfaction influences organizational commitment, which then affects employee turnover. As Figure 2.1 depicts, the interaction of the individual and the job determines levels of job satisfaction and organizational commitment. "Loyal" employees are more than just satisfied with their jobs; they are pleased with the relationship with their employers.

Organizational commitment is the degree to which employees believe in and accept organizational goals and desire to remain with the organization. A related

FIGURE 2.1   Factors Affecting Job Satisfaction and Organizational Commitment

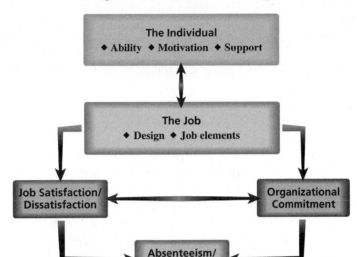

idea is *employee engagement,* which is the extent to which an employee is willing and able to contribute.

A logical extension of organizational commitment focuses more specifically on *continuance commitment* factors, which suggests that decisions to remain with or leave an organization ultimately are reflected in employee absenteeism and turnover statistics. Individuals who are not as satisfied with their jobs or who are not as committed to the organization are more likely to withdraw from the organization. Absenteeism is temporary withdrawal, while turnover is permanent.

EMPLOYEE ABSENTEEISM

Absenteeism is any failure to report for work as scheduled or to stay at work when scheduled. The cause does not matter when counting someone absent. Absenteeism is expensive, costing an estimated $645 per employee each year.[3]

Types of Absenteeism

Employees can be absent from work for several reasons. Clearly, some absenteeism is inevitable because illness, death in the family, and other personal reasons for absences are unavoidable and understandable. Many employers have sick leave policies that allow employees a certain number of paid days each year for these types of *involuntary* absences. However, much absenteeism is avoidable, or *voluntary.* Often, a relatively small number of individuals are responsible for a disproportionate share of the total absenteeism in an organization.

HR Metrics: Measuring Absenteeism

Controlling or reducing absenteeism must begin with continuous monitoring of the absenteeism statistics in work units. Such monitoring helps managers pinpoint employees who are frequently absent and departments that have excessive absenteeism. Various methods of measuring or computing absenteeism exist. One formula suggested by the U.S. Department of Labor is as follows:

$$\text{Number of person-days lost through job absence during period} / (\text{Average number of employees}) \times (\text{Number of workdays}) \times 100$$

(This rate can also be based on number of hours instead of number of days.)

Controlling Absenteeism

Voluntary absenteeism is easiest to control if managers clearly understand its causes. Once they do, they can use a variety of approaches to reduce it. Organizational policies on absenteeism should be stated clearly in an employee handbook and stressed by supervisors and managers. Approaches to control absenteeism fall into several categories:

▶ *Disciplinary approach:* Many employers use a disciplinary approach. People who are absent the first time receive an oral warning, and subsequent absences bring written warnings, suspension, and finally dismissal.

▶ *Positive reinforcement:* Positive reinforcement includes such methods as giving employees cash, recognition, time off, or other rewards for meeting attendance standards.

▶ *Combination approach:* A combination approach ideally rewards desired behaviors and punishes undesired behaviors. This "carrot and stick" approach uses policies and discipline to punish offenders, and various programs and rewards to recognize employees with outstanding attendance.

▶ *"No fault" policy:* With a "no fault" policy, the reasons for absences do not matter, and the employees must manage their own attendance unless they abuse that freedom. Once absenteeism exceeds normal limits, then disciplinary action up to and including termination of employment can occur.

▶ *Paid-time-off (PTO) programs:* Some employers have paid-time-off programs, in which vacation time, holidays, and sick leave for each employee are combined into a PTO account. Employees use days from their accounts at their discretion for illness, personal time, or vacation.

EMPLOYEE TURNOVER

Like absenteeism, turnover is related to job satisfaction and organizational commitment. **Turnover** occurs when employees leave an organization and have to be replaced.

Many organizations have found that turnover is a costly problem, as documented by a number of studies. In many service industries, the turnover rates and costs are very high. Turnover costs are certainly not unique to the United States. Articles have described turnover in the call centers located in India—a problem similar to that faced by the industry in the United States.[4]

Types of Turnover

Turnover is classified in a number of ways. Each of the following classifications can be used, and the two are not mutually exclusive:

► **Involuntary Turnover**

Employees are terminated for poor performance or work rule violations

► **Voluntary Turnover**

Employees leave by choice

Involuntary turnover is triggered by organizational policies, work rules, and performance standards that are not met by employees.

► **Functional Turnover**

Lower-performing or disruptive employees leave

► **Dysfunctional Turnover**

Key individuals and high performers leave at critical times

Not all turnover is negative for organizations; on the contrary, some workforce losses are desirable, especially if those who leave are lower-performing, less reliable individuals, or disrupt coworkers. Unfortunately for organizations, dysfunctional turnover does occur. That happens when key individuals leave, often at crucial work times.

► **Uncontrollable Turnover**

Employees leave for reasons outside the control of the employer

► **Controllable Turnover**

Employees leave for reasons that could be influenced by the employer

Employees quit for many reasons that cannot be controlled by the organization. These reasons include (1) the employee moves out of the geographic area, (2) the employee decides to stay home with young children or elder relatives, (3) the employee's spouse is transferred, and (4) the employee is a student worker who graduates from college. Even though some turnover is inevitable, many employers today must address turnover that is controllable. Organizations are better able to retain employees if they deal with the concerns of employees that are leading to turnover.

HR METRICS: Measuring Turnover

The turnover rate for an organization can be computed in different ways. The following formula from the U.S. Department of Labor is widely used; in it, the term *separations* means departures from the organization.

$$\text{Number of employee separations during the month} / \text{Total number of employees at midmonth} \times 100$$

Common turnover rates range from almost 0% to more than 100% a year and vary among industries. Often a part of HR management systems, turnover data can be gathered and analyzed in a number of different ways, including the following categories:

- Job and job level
- Department, unit, and location
- Reason for leaving
- Length of service

- Demographic characteristics
- Education and training
- Knowledge, skills, and abilities
- Performance ratings/levels

Determining Turnover Costs Determining turnover costs can be relatively simple or very complex, depending on the nature of the efforts and data used. Some of the most common areas considered include the following:

- *Separation costs:* Includes HR staff and supervisor time and salaries to prevent separations, exit interview time, unemployment expenses, legal fees for separations challenged, accrued vacation, continued benefits, etc.
- *Replacement costs:* Includes recruiting and advertising expenses, search fees, HR interviewer and staff time and salaries, employee referral fees, relocation and moving costs, supervisor and managerial time and salaries, employment testing costs, reference checking fees, preemployment medical expenses, etc.
- *Training costs:* Includes paid orientation time, training staff time and salaries, costs of training materials, supervisors' and managers' time and salaries, coworker "coaching" time and salaries, etc.
- *Hidden costs:* Includes costs not obvious but that affect lost productivity, decreased customer service, other employee turnover, missed deadlines, etc.

INDIVIDUAL EMPLOYEE PERFORMANCE

The HR unit in an organization exists in part to analyze and address the performance of individual employees. Exactly how that should be done depends on what upper management expects. Like any management function, HR management activities should be developed, evaluated, and changed as necessary so that they can contribute to the competitive performance of the individuals at work and therefore of the organization.

Individual Performance Factors

The three major factors that affect a given individual's performance are: (1) individual ability to do the work, (2) effort expended, and (3) organizational support. The relationship of these factors is widely acknowledged in management literature as follows:

$$\text{Performance } (P) = \text{Ability } (A) \times \text{Effort } (E) \times \text{Support } (S)$$

Individual performance is enhanced to the degree that all three components are present with an individual employee, and diminished if any of these factors is reduced or absent. Individual motivation, one of the variables that affects effort, is often missing from the performance equation.

Individual Motivation

Motivation is the desire within a person causing that person to act. People usually act for one reason: to reach a goal. Thus, motivation is a goal-directed drive, and it seldom occurs in a void. The words *need, want, desire,* and *drive* are all similar to *motive,* from which the word *motivation* is derived. Understanding motivation is important because performance, reaction to compensation, turnover, and other HR concerns are affected by and influence motivation.

Management Implications for Motivating Individual Performance

Motivation is complex and individualized, and managerial strategies and tactics must be broadbased to address the motivation concerns of individuals. For instance, managers must determine whether inadequate individual behavior is due to employee deficiencies, inconsistent reward policies, or low desire for the rewards offered. Additionally, managers may try training to improve employee performance or look at the methods by which they appraise and reward performance.

In summary, answering the question often asked by managers, "How do I motivate my employees?" requires managerial diagnoses of employees' efforts, abilities, and expectations. For that reason, the relationships between individuals and their organizations are an integral part of effective HR management, and affect employee retention.

RETENTION OF HUMAN RESOURCES

Retention must be viewed as a strategic business issue. Companies are being forced to study why employees leave and why they stay. While experts can (and do) make some observations, each organization must determine the causes for its own specific retention situation.

The characteristics of the "stay or go" decision are personal and not entirely within the control of an employer. However, there are factors related to those individual decisions that an employer *can* control. Figure 2.2 shows those factors, and also indicates that they are "drivers" of retention, or forces that an employer can manage to improve retention.

Characteristics of the Employer and Retention

A number of organizational characteristics influence individuals in their decisions to stay with or leave their employers. Organizations experience less turnover when they have positive, distinctive cultures; effective management; and recognizable job security.

Organizational culture is a pattern of shared values and beliefs of a workforce. These items provide organizational members with meaning and rules for behavior.

FIGURE 2.2 Drivers of Retention

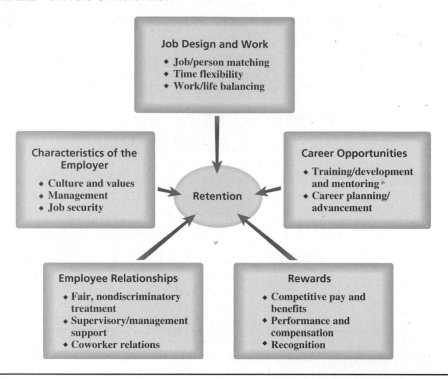

One corporation well known for its culture and values is Southwest Airlines. The firm focuses considerable HR efforts on instilling its values of customer service and employee involvement. These efforts have yielded greater performance, retention of employees, and a reputation as an "employer of choice" in the airline industry.

Other organizational components that affect employee retention are related to the management of the organization. Some organizations see external events as threatening, whereas others see changes as challenges requiring responses. The latter approach can be a source of competitive advantage, especially if an organization is in a growing, dynamic industry. The attitudes and approaches of management are the key.

Job Security is another concern because many individuals have seen a decline in job security over the past decade. All the downsizings, layoffs, mergers and acquisitions, and organizational restructurings have affected employee loyalty and retention. Also, as coworkers experience layoffs and job reductions, the anxiety levels of the remaining employees rise. But job security is not solely about one's personal security. A major issue in retention is the extent to which high-caliber top performers are retained by the company. Other employees view high turnover in this group and the company as a negative in the retention equation.[5]

Job Design, Work and Retention

Job design refers to organizing tasks, duties, and responsibilities into a productive unit of work. It addresses the content of jobs and the effect of jobs on employees. Identifying the components of a given job is an integral part of job design. Currently, job design is receiving greater attention for three major reasons:

▶ Job design can influence *performance* in certain jobs, especially those where employee motivation can make a substantial difference. Lower costs resulting from reduced turnover and absenteeism also are related to the effective design of jobs.
▶ Job design can affect *job satisfaction*. Because people are more satisfied with certain job configurations than with others, identifying what makes a "good" job becomes critical.
▶ Job design can affect both *physical* and *mental health*. Problems such as hearing loss, backache, and leg pain sometimes can be traced directly to job design, as can stress, high blood pressure, and heart disease.

The **person/job fit** is a simple but important concept of matching characteristics of people with characteristics of jobs. If a person does not fit a job, either the person can be changed or replaced, or the job can be altered. In the past, it was much more common to try to make the "round" person fit the "square" job.

But, it is hard to successfully reshape people. By redesigning jobs, the person/job fit may be improved more easily. Improving the person/job fit may affect individual responses to jobs because a job may be motivating to one person but not to someone else. One tactic for designing or redesigning jobs is to simplify the job tasks and responsibilities. Job simplification may be appropriate for jobs that are to be staffed with entry-level employees. However, making jobs too simple may result in boring jobs that appeal to few people, causing high turnover. Several different approaches are useful as part of job design, including job enlargement, job enrichment, and job rotation.

Using Teams in Jobs Typically, a job is thought of as something done by one person. However, where it is appropriate jobs may be designed for teams. In an attempt to make jobs more meaningful and to take advantage of the increased productivity and commitment that can follow such a change, more organizations are assigning jobs to teams of employees instead of individuals. Some firms have gone as far as dropping such terms as workers and employees, replacing them with teammates, crew members, associates, and other titles that emphasize teamwork.

With more firms operating globally, the use of global teams has increased significantly. Many times, members of global teams never or seldom meet in person. Instead, they "meet" electronically, using Web-based systems.[6]

Teams are more likely to be successful if they are allowed to function with sufficient authority to make decisions about their activities and operations. As a transition to work teams occurs, significant efforts are necessary to define the areas, scope of authority, and goals of the teams. Additionally, teams must recognize and address dissent and conflict. Contrary to what some might believe, suppressing dissent and conflict to preserve harmony ultimately becomes destructive to the effective operation of a team.

Job Design, Work Schedules, And Telework

A job consists of the tasks an employee does, the relationships required on the job, the tools the employee works with, and many other elements. Considerations that increasingly affect job design for both employers and employees are the time during which work is scheduled and the location of employees when working.

The pressures of employees' lives, coupled with the demands of their jobs, can lead to emotional imbalances that are collectively labeled *stress*. The main causes of job-related stress appear to be time pressures, fears of losing a job, deadlines, and fragmented work. To respond to stress and other concerns, employers are using different work schedule alternatives, flexible scheduling, and telework.

Work Schedules   The work schedules associated with different jobs vary. Some jobs must be performed during "normal" daily work hours and workdays, and some jobs require working nights, weekends, and extended hours.

Flexible work schedules allow organizations to make better use of workers by matching work demands to work hours. One type of flexible scheduling is **flextime,** in which employees work a set number of hours a day but vary starting and ending times. Some firms allow employees to work reduced schedules and receive proportional wages/salaries. Certain levels of hours are worked weekly or monthly.

Flexible scheduling allows management to relax some of the traditional "time clock" control of employees, while still covering workloads. In the United States, over 30% of the full-time workforce vary their work hours from those in the traditional model, more than double the rate a decade ago. Also, over 60% of workers surveyed indicated that they had complete or some control over their work schedules.[7]

Job Sharing   Another alternative used to add flexibility and more work-life balancing is **job sharing,** in which two employees perform the work of one full-time job. For instance, a hospital allows two radiological technicians to fill one job, whereby each individual works every other week. Such arrangements are beneficial for employees who may not want to or be able to work full-time because of family, school, or other reasons. Job sharing also can be effective because each person can substitute for the other when illness, vacation, or other circumstances occur. The key to successful job sharing is that both "job sharers" work effectively together and each is competent in meeting the job requirements.

Telework   The developments in information and communications technology mean that employees can work anywhere and anytime. As a result, a growing number of employers are allowing employees to work from widely varied locations.

Some employees *telecommute,* which means they work via electronic computing and telecommunications equipment. Many U.S. employers have employees who telecommute one or more days a week.

Work/Life Balancing Balancing the demands of work with the responsibilities of life, including family and personal responsibilities, is a challenge; some may say it is an impossibility. Work/life balancing programs commonly used include:

- Different work arrangements
- Leave for children's school functions
- Compressed workweek
- Job sharing
- On-site child/adult care

- Telecommuting
- Employee assistance plans
- On-site health services
- Wellness programs
- Fitness facility

Career Opportunities and Retention

Surveys of workers in all types of jobs consistently indicate that organizational efforts to aid career development can significantly affect employee retention. Such surveys have found that *opportunities for personal growth* lead the list of reasons why individuals took their current jobs and why they stay there. This component is even more essential for technical professionals and those under age 35, for whom opportunities to develop skills and obtain promotions rank above compensation as a retention concern.

Organizations also increase employee retention through formal career planning efforts. Employees discuss with their managers career opportunities within the organization and career development activities that will help the employees grow. Career development and planning efforts may include formal mentoring programs. Also, companies can reduce attrition by showing employees that they are serious about promoting from within.

Rewards and Retention

The tangible rewards that people receive for working come in the form of pay, incentives, and benefits. Numerous surveys and experiences of HR professionals reveal that one key to retention is having *competitive compensation practices.* Many managers believe that money is the prime retention factor. Often, employees cite better pay or higher compensation as a reason for leaving one employer for another. However, the reality is a bit more complex.

Competitive Pay and Benefits Pay and benefits *must be competitive,* which means they must be close to what other employers are providing and what individuals believe to be consistent with their capabilities, experience, and performance. If compensation is not close, often defined as within 10% of the "market" rate, then turnover is likely to be higher.

Performance and Compensation Many individuals expect their rewards to be differentiated from those of others based on performance. That means, for instance, that if an employee receives about the same pay increase and overall pay as others who produce less, are absent more, and work fewer hours, then that person may feel that the situation is "unfair." This may prompt the individual to look for another job where compensation recognizes performance differences. To strengthen links between organizational and individual performance, a growing number of private-sector firms are using variable pay and incentives programs. These programs offer cash bonuses or lump-sum payments to reward extra performance.

Recognition Employee recognition as a form of reward can be either tangible or intangible. Tangible recognition comes in many forms, such as "employee of the month" plaques and perfect-attendance certificates. Intangible and psychological recognition includes feedback from managers and supervisors that acknowledges extra effort and performance, even if monetary rewards are not given.

Employee Relationships and Retention

A final set of factors found to affect retention is based on the relationships that employees have in organizations. Such areas as the reasonableness of HR policies, the fairness of disciplinary actions, and the means used to decide work assignments and opportunities all affect employee retention. If individuals feel that policies are unreasonably restrictive or are applied inconsistently, then they may be more likely to look at jobs offered by other employers.[8]

The increasing demographic diversity of U.S. workplaces makes *fair* and *nondiscriminatory treatment* of employees, regardless of gender, age, and other characteristics, particularly important. Other relationships that affect employee retention are *supervisory/management support* and *coworker relations*.

MANAGING RETENTION

The foregoing section summarized the results of many studies and HR practices to identify factors that can cause retention difficulties. Now the focus turns to what a manager can do about retention issues. Figure 2.3 shows the keys to managing retention.

Retention Measurement and Assessment

To ensure that appropriate actions are taken to enhance retention, management decisions require data and analyses rather than subjective impressions, anecdotes of selected individual situations, or panic reactions to the loss of key people. Having several *absence and turnover measurements* to analyze is important. Two other sources of information might be useful before analysis is done: employee surveys and exit interviews.

Employee Surveys Employee surveys can be used to diagnose specific problem areas, identify employee needs or preferences, and reveal areas in which HR

FIGURE 2.3   Keys to Managing Retention

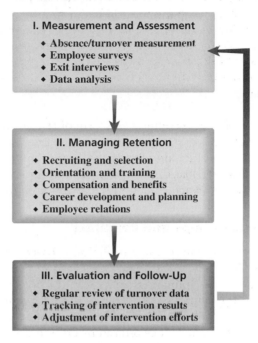

activities are well received or are viewed negatively. Obtaining employee input provides managers and HR professionals with data on the "retention climate" in an organization.

Exit Interviews   One widely used type of interview is the **exit interview,** in which individuals are asked to give their reasons for leaving the organization. Many employers conduct exit interviews, and half use the information gathered to make changes to aid retention. A wide range of issues can be examined in exit interviews.

Determining Retention Management Actions

The analysis of data mined from turnover and absenteeism records, surveys of employees, and exit interviews is an attempt to get at the cause of retention problems. There are numerous actions management might take to deal with retention issues. The choice of a particular action depends on the analysis of the turnover and retention problems in a particular organization and should be custom-tailored for that organization.

Retention Evaluation and Follow-Up

Once appropriate management actions have been implemented, it is important that they be evaluated and that appropriate follow-up be conducted and adjustments made. *Regular review of turnover data* can identify when turnover increases or decreases among different employee groups classified by length of service, education, department, and gender, etc. *Tracking of intervention results* and *adjustment of intervention efforts* also should be part of evaluation efforts.

NOTES

1. Jeffery Thompson and J. Stuart Bunderson, "Violations of Principle: Ideological Currency in the Psychological Contract," *Academy of Management Review*, 28 (2003), 571–586.

2. "As Job Satisfaction Declines Further, Demands on Workers Rise, Surveys Say," *Bulletin to Management*, October 2, 2003, 314.

3. "2003 CCH Unscheduled Absence Survey," CCH Incorporated, November 4, 2003, 1.

4. Joanna Slater, "Attrition Besets India Call Centers," *Wall Street Journal*, December 31, 2003, A8.

5. Steve Bates, "Getting Engaged," *HR Magazine*, February 2004, 44–51.

6. P. Christopher Earley and Cristina B. Gibson, *Multinational Work Teams* (Mahwah, NJ: Lawrence Erlbaum Associates, 2002).

7. Families and Work Institute, 2002, *http://www.familiesandwork.org*.

8. David Jones and Daniel Skarlicki, "The Relationship Between Perceptions of Fairness and Voluntary Turnover Among Retail Employees," *Journal of Applied Social Psychology*, 33 (2003), 1226–1243.

INTERNET RESOURCES

Talent Keepers   This organization offers Web-based employee retention ideas. **http://www.talentkeepers.com**

You Can Work from Anywhere   One of the resources here is a tab on work/life balance that links to other useful sites. **http://www.youcanworkfromanywhere.com**

SUGGESTED READINGS

Kathleen G. Connolly and Paul M. Connolly, *Employee Opinion Questionnaires,* (New York: John Wiley & Sons, 2004

Alan J. Dubinsky and Steven J. Skinner, *High Performers: Recruiting and Retaining Top Employees* (Mason, OH: Thomson Learning, 2003).

Jack S. Phillips, *Retaining Your Best Employees* (Alexandria, VA: ASTD/SHRM, 2002).

Michael Watkins, *Intrinsic Motivation at Work* (San Francisco, CA: Berrett-Koehler, 2002).

Chapter 3

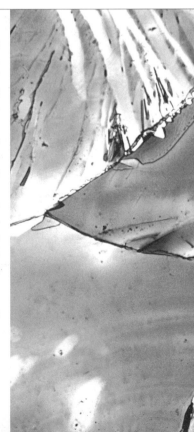

Equal Employment

EQUAL EMPLOYMENT OPPORTUNITY CONCEPTS

Managerial Perspectives on HR

1. What are the basic concepts employers should follow to ensure equal employment compliance?

2. Why must employers in the United States learn to adjust to diversity if they are to be effective in the future?

3. What must be addressed to prevent discrimination based on gender/sex and disabilities issues?

Equal employment opportunity (EEO) is the concept that all individuals should have equal treatment in all employment-related actions. Initial concerns were especially with hiring, firing, pay, and promotion based on gender, religion, and race. But the idea spread to include age, pregnancy, and the disabled.

Not everyone agrees on the best way to achieve equal employment opportunity. There seems to be little disagreement that the goal is **equal employment,** or employment that is not affected by illegal discrimination. The word *discrimination* simply means "recognizing differences among items or people." For example, employers must discriminate (choose) among applicants for a job on the basis of job requirements and candidates' qualifications. However, discrimination is illegal in employment-related situations in which either (1) different standards are used to judge different individuals, or (2) the same standard is used, but it is not related to the individuals' jobs. Charges of illegal discrimination continue to be filed, indicating that employers still do not deal with people fairly all the time.[1]

Various laws have been passed to protect individuals who share certain characteristics, such as race, age, or gender. Those having the designated characteristics are referred to as a **protected class,** which is composed of individuals who fall within a group identified for protection under equal employment laws and regulations. The following bases for protection have been identified by various federal, state, and/or local laws:

▶ Race, ethnic origin, color (African Americans, Hispanic Americans, Native Americans, Asian Americans)
▶ Sex/gender (women, including those who are pregnant)

- ▶ Age (individuals over age 40)
- ▶ Individuals with disabilities (physical or mental)
- ▶ Military experience (Vietnam-era veterans)
- ▶ Religion (special beliefs and practices)
- ▶ Marital status (some states)
- ▶ Sexual orientation (some states and cities)

MAJOR EQUAL EMPLOYMENT LAWS

Even if an organization has little regard for the principles of equal employment opportunity, it must follow federal, state, and local EEO laws and some affirmative action regulations to avoid costly penalties. Numerous federal, state, and local laws address equal employment opportunity concerns, as shown in Appendix A. An overview of the major laws, regulations, and concepts follows.

Civil Rights Act of 1964, Title VII

Although the first civil rights act was passed in 1866, but it was not until passage of the Civil Rights Act of 1964 that the keystone of antidiscrimination employment legislation was put into place. The Equal Employment Opportunity Commission (EEOC) was established to enforce the provisions of Title VII, the portion of the act that deals with employment.

Title VII covers most employers in the United States. Any organization meeting one of the criteria in the following list is subject to rules and regulations that specific government agencies have established to administer the act:

- ▶ All private employers of 15 or more persons who are employed 20 or more weeks a year
- ▶ All educational institutions, public and private
- ▶ State and local governments
- ▶ Public and private employment agencies
- ▶ Labor unions with 15 or more members
- ▶ Joint labor/management committees for apprenticeships and training

Title VII has been the basis for several extensions of EEO laws. For example, in 1980, the EEOC interpreted the law to include sexual harassment. Further, a number of concepts identified in Title VII are the foundation for court decisions, regulations, and other laws discussed later in the chapter. Some of those concepts are depicted in Figure 3.1.

EEO Concepts As has been emphasized by regulations and court decisions, employers are expected to use job-related employment practices. A **business necessity** is a practice necessary for safe and efficient organizational operations. Business necessity has been the subject of numerous court decisions. Educational requirements often are based on business necessity. However, an employer who requires a minimum level of education, such as a high school diploma, must be able to defend the requirement as essential to the performance of the job.

FIGURE 3.1   EEO Concepts

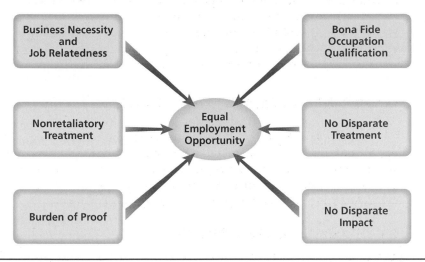

A **bona fide occupational qualification (BFOQ)** is a characteristic providing a legitimate reason why an employer can exclude persons on otherwise illegal bases of consideration. What constitutes a BFOQ has been subject to different interpretations in various courts across the United States. Legal uses of BFOQs have been found for hiring Asians to wait on customers in a Chinese restaurant or Catholics to serve in certain religious-based positions in Catholic churches.

Disparate treatment occurs when members of a protected class are treated differently from others. For example, if female applicants must take a special skills test not given to male applicants, then disparate treatment may be occurring. If disparate treatment has occurred, the courts generally have indicated that intentional discrimination exists.

Disparate impact occurs when members of a protected class are substantially underrepresented as a result of employment decisions that work to their disadvantage. The landmark case that established the importance of disparate impact as a legal foundation of EEO law is *Griggs v. Duke Power* (1971).[2]

Another legal issue that arises when discrimination is alleged is the determination of which party has the **burden of proof,** which is what individuals who file suit against employers must prove in order to establish that illegal discrimination has occurred.

Based on the evolution of court decisions, current laws and regulations state that the plaintiff charging discrimination (1) must be a *protected-class member* and (2) must prove that *disparate impact* or *disparate treatment* existed. Once a court rules that a *prima facie* (preliminary) case has been made, the burden of proof shifts to the employer. The employer then must show that the bases for making employment-related decisions were specifically job related and consistent with considerations of business necessity.

Employers are prohibited by EEO laws from retaliating against individuals who file discrimination charges. **Retaliation** occurs when employers take punitive actions against individuals who exercise their legal rights.

Civil Rights Act of 1991

The Civil Rights Act of 1991 requires employers to show that an employment practice is *job related for the position* and is consistent with *business necessity*. The act clarifies that the plaintiffs bringing the discrimination charges must identify the particular employer practice being challenged and must show only that protected-class status played *some role*. For employers, this requirement means that an individual's race, color, religion, sex, or national origin *must play no role* in their employment practices.

Executive Orders 11246, 11375, and 11478

The changing laws over the last 30 years have forced employers to address additional areas of potential discrimination. Several acts and regulations apply specifically to government contractors. These acts and regulations specify a minimum number of employees and size of government contracts. The requirements primarily come from federal Executive Orders 11246, 11375, and 11478. Many states have similar requirements for firms with state government contracts.

Affirmative Action

Affirmative action regulations are a requirement for federal government contractors to document the inclusion of women and racial minorities in the workforce. As part of these government regulations, covered employers must submit plans describing their attempts to narrow the gaps between the composition of their workforces and the composition of labor markets where they obtain employees. Generally, the courts have upheld the legality of affirmative action, but recently they have limited it somewhat.[3] One major case involved a University of Michigan policy of allotting every minority applicant 20 out of the 150 points necessary to guarantee admission. The U.S. Supreme Court held that the system violated the Fourteenth Amendment's "equal protection" clause. However, in another case, the court upheld affirmative action, ruling that the University of Michigan law school was justified in trying to ensure that a "critical mass" of minority students was admitted, even if that meant denying admission to white students with better grades or higher test scores.

Affirmative Action Plans Federal, state, and local regulations require many government contractors to compile affirmative action plans to report on the composition of their workforces. An **affirmative action plan (AAP)** is a formal document that an employer compiles annually for submission to enforcement agencies. Generally, contractors with at least 50 employees and $50,000 in government contracts annually must submit these plans. A crucial but time-consuming part of an AAP is making two types of analyses and comparisons. The **availability analysis** identifies the number of protected-class members available to work in the appropriate labor markets for given jobs. This analysis can be developed with data from a state labor department, the U.S. Census Bureau, and other sources. The **utilization analysis** identifies the number of protected-class members employed in the organization and the types of jobs they hold.

Government agencies at several levels can investigate illegal discriminatory practices. At the federal level, the two most prominent agencies are the Equal Employment Opportunity Commission and the Office of Federal Contract Compliance Programs.

In addition to federal laws and orders, many states and municipalities have passed their own laws prohibiting discrimination on a variety of bases, and state and local enforcement bodies have been established. Compared with federal laws, state and local laws sometimes provide greater remedies, require different actions or prohibit discrimination in more areas.

Uniform Guidelines on Employee Selection Procedures

The 1978 Uniform Guidelines on Employee Selection Procedures are used by the U.S. EEOC, the U.S. Department of Labor's OFCCP, the U.S. Department of Justice, and the U.S. Office of Personnel Management. These guidelines attempt to explain how an employer should deal with hiring, retention, promotion, transfer, demotion, dismissal, and referral. Under the uniform guidelines, if sued, employers can choose one of two routes to prove they are not illegally discriminating against employees: no disparate impact, and job-related validity.

"No Disparate Impact" Approach Generally, the most important issue regarding discrimination in organizations is the *effect* of employment policies and procedures, regardless of the *intent* of the employer. *Disparate impact* occurs when protected-class members are substantially underrepresented in employment decisions. Under the guidelines, disparate impact is determined with the **4/5ths rule.** If the selection rate for a protected group is less than 80% (4/5ths) of the selection rate for the majority group or less than 80% of the majority group's representation in the relevant labor market, discrimination exists. Thus, the guidelines have attempted to define discrimination in statistical terms. Disparate impact should be checked by employers both internally and externally.

Job-Related Validation Approach Under the job-related validation approach, virtually every factor used to make employment-related decisions—recruiting, selection, promotion, termination, discipline, and performance appraisal—must be shown to be job related. Hence, the concept of validity affects many of the common tools used to make HR decisions.

Validity is simply the extent to which a test actually measures what it says it measures. The concept relates to inferences made from tests. Ideally, employment-related tests will be both valid and reliable. **Reliability** refers to the consistency with which a test measures an item. For a test to be reliable, an individual's score should be about the same every time the individual takes the test (allowing for the effects of practice).

VALIDITY AND EQUAL EMPLOYMENT

There are two types of validation strategies: content validity and criterion-related validity (concurrent and predictive). **Content validity** is validity measured by a logical, nonstatistical method to identify the KSAs and other characteristics necessary to perform a job. A test has content validity if it reflects an actual sample of the work done on the job in question.

Employment tests attempt to predict how well an individual will perform on the job. In measuring **criterion-related validity,** a test is the *predictor,* and the measures for job performance are the *criterion variables.* (See Figure 3.2.) Job analysis determines as exactly as possible what KSAs and behaviors are needed for each task in the job.

There are two approaches to criterion-related validity. *Concurrent validity* is an "at-the-same-time" approach, and *predictive validity* is a "before-the-fact" approach. Figure 3.2 depicts both.

FIGURE 3.2 Concurrent and Predictive Validity

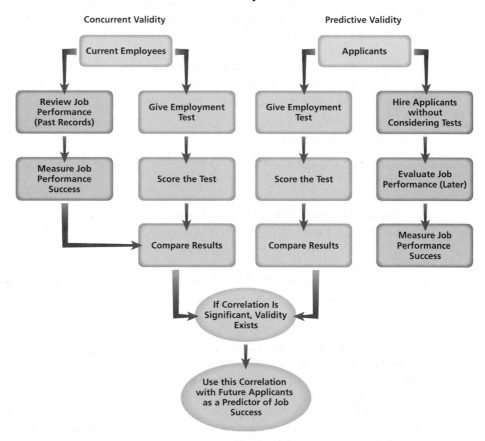

EEO COMPLIANCE

Employers must comply with a variety of EEO regulations and guidelines. To do so, management should have an EEO policy statement and maintain all of the required EEO-related records. All employers with 15 or more employees are required to keep certain records. All employment records must be maintained as required. Such records include application forms and documents concerning hiring, promotion, demotion, transfer, layoff, termination, rates of pay or other terms of compensation, and selection for training and apprenticeship. Even application forms or test papers completed by unsuccessful applicants may be requested. The length of time that documents must be kept varies, but generally *three years is recommended as a minimum.* Complete records are necessary to enable an employer to respond, should a charge of discrimination be made. Also, a basic report that must be filed with the EEOC is the annual report form EEO-1.

Under EEO laws and regulations, employers may be required to show that they do not discriminate in the recruiting and selection of members of protected classes. Because employers are not allowed to collect such data on application blanks and other preemployment records, the EEOC allows them to do so with a "visual" survey or a separate applicant-flow form that is not used in the selection process. The applicant-flow form is filled out voluntarily by the applicant, and that data must be maintained separately from other selection-related materials.

When a discrimination complaint is received by the EEOC or a similar agency, it must be processed. Figure 3.3 shows the employer's responses to an EEO complaint.

Sex/Gender Discrimination

A number of laws and regulations address discrimination on the bases of sex/gender; an overview follows.

Pregnancy Discrimination Act The Pregnancy Discrimination Act (PDA) of 1978 requires that any employer with 15 or more employees treat maternity leave the same as other personal or medical leaves. Closely related to the PDA is the Family and Medical Leave Act (FMLA) of 1993, which requires that individuals be given up to 12 weeks of family leave without pay and also requires that those taking family leave be allowed to return to jobs. The FMLA applies to both men and women.

Equal Pay and Pay Equity The Equal Pay Act of 1963 requires employers to pay similar wage rates for similar work without regard to gender. A *common core of tasks* must be similar, but tasks performed only intermittently or infrequently do not make jobs different enough to justify significantly different wages. Differences in pay may be allowed because of (1) differences in seniority, (2) differences in performance, (3) differences in quality and/or quantity of production, and (4) factors other than sex, such as skill, effort, and working conditions.

FIGURE 3.3 **Stages in the Employer's Response to an EEO Complaint**

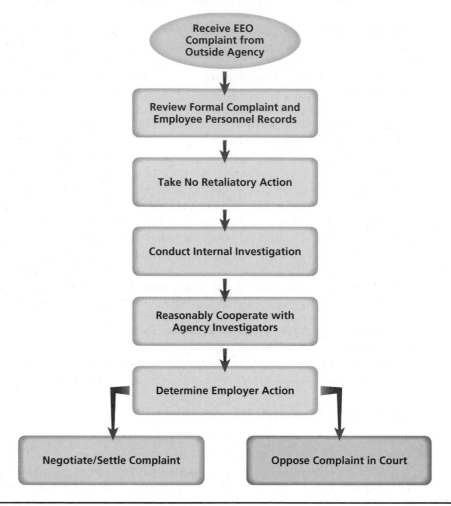

Pay equity is the idea that the pay for jobs requiring comparable levels of knowledge, skill, and ability should be similar, even if actual duties differ significantly. This theory has also been called *comparable worth* in earlier cases. But except where state laws have mandated pay equity for public-sector employees, U.S. federal courts generally have ruled that the existence of pay differences between jobs held by women and jobs held by men is not sufficient to prove that illegal discrimination has occurred.

Sexual Harassment The Equal Employment Opportunity Commission has issued guidelines designed to curtail sexual harassment. **Sexual harassment** refers to actions that are sexually directed, are unwanted, and subject the worker to adverse employment conditions or create a hostile work environment. Sexual harassment can occur between a boss and a subordinate, among coworkers, and when nonemployees have business contacts with employees.[4]

Glass Ceiling   For years, women's groups have alleged that women in workplaces encounter a glass ceiling, which refers to discriminatory practices that have prevented women and other protected-class members from advancing to executive-level jobs. Women in the United States are making some progress; today, overall, 39% of women are in managerial or professional jobs, up from 24% in 1977.[5]

Types of Sexual Harassment   Two basic types of sexual harassment have been defined by EEOC regulations and a large number of court cases. The two types are different in nature and defined as follows: (1) **Quid pro quo** is harassment in which employment outcomes are linked to the individual granting sexual favors. (2) **Hostile environment** harassment exists when an individual's work performance or psychological well-being is unreasonably affected by intimidating or offensive working conditions. Regardless of the type of sexual harassment, it is apparent that sexual harassment has significant consequences on the organization, other employees and especially those harassed. Only if the employer can produce evidence of an affirmative defense in which the employer took reasonable care to prohibit sexual harassment does the employer have the possibility of avoiding liability. Critical components of ensuring reasonable care include the following:

► Establishing a sexual harassment policy
► Communicating the policy regularly
► Training employees and managers on avoiding sexual harassment
► Investigating and taking action when complaints are voiced

Americans with Disabilities Act

The passage of the Americans with Disabilities Act (ADA) in 1990 expanded the scope and impact of laws and regulations on discrimination against individuals with disabilities. The ADA affects more than just employment matters. All employers with 15 or more employees are covered by the provisions of the ADA, which are enforced by the EEOC, and the act applies to private employers, employment agencies, and labor unions. State government employees are not covered by the ADA, which means that they cannot sue in federal courts for redress and damages. However, they may still bring suits under state laws in state courts.

Who Is Disabled?   As defined by the ADA, a **disabled** person is someone who has a physical or mental impairment that substantially limits that person in some major life activities, who has a record of such an impairment, or who is regarded as having such an impairment. In spite of the EEOC guidelines, some confusion still remains as to who is disabled. A growing area of concern under the ADA is individuals with mental disabilities. A mental illness is often more difficult to diagnose than a physical disability. Employers must be careful when considering "emotional" or "mental health" factors such as depression in employment-related decisions. They must not stereotype individuals with mental disabilities, but base their evaluations on sound medical information.[6]

ADA and Job Requirements The ADA contains a number of specific requirements that deal with employment of individuals with disabilities. Discrimination is prohibited against individuals with disabilities who can perform the **essential job functions**—the fundamental job duties—of the employment positions that those individuals hold or desire. These functions do not include marginal functions of the position. For a qualified person with a disability, an employer must make a **reasonable accommodation,** which is a modification or adjustment to a job or work environment that gives that individual an equal employment opportunity. EEOC guidelines encourage employers and individuals to work together to determine what are appropriate reasonable accommodations, rather than employers alone making those judgments.

Reasonable accommodation is restricted to actions that do not place an undue hardship on an employer. An **undue hardship** is a significant difficulty or expense imposed on an employer in making an accommodation for individuals with disabilities. The ADA offers only general guidelines in determining when an accommodation becomes unreasonable and places undue hardship on an employer. Most accommodation expenditures by employers have been relatively modest.[7] The ADA also contains restrictions on obtaining and retaining medically related information on applicants and employees. Restrictions include prohibiting employers from rejecting an individual because of a disability and from asking job applicants any question about current or past medical history until a conditional job offer is made.

AGE, RACE, AND OTHER TYPES OF DISCRIMINATION

Several other types of discrimination have been identified as illegal. A growing number of issues in the various areas of discrimination require attention by employers.

Age Discrimination

The Age Discrimination in Employment Act (ADEA) of 1967, amended, prohibits discrimination in terms, conditions, or privileges of employment against all individuals age 40 or older working for employers having 20 or more workers. However, the U.S. Supreme Court has ruled that state employees may not sue state government employers in federal courts because the ADEA is a federal law.

The Supreme Court ruled that while older workers can sue if they are not treated the same as younger workers, the reverse is *not* true. Two hundred General Dynamics employees had sued because they were too young to get benefits offered to colleagues age 50 and over. The workers (who were all in their 40s) argued reverse discrimination and lost.

Older Workers Benefit Protection Act (OWBPA) This law is an amendment to the ADEA and is aimed at protecting employees when they sign liability waivers for age discrimination in exchange for severance packages. For example, an early retirement package that includes a waiver stating the employee will not sue for age discrimination if he or she takes the money for early retirement must meet certain provisions.

Immigration Reform and Control Acts The Immigration Reform and Control Acts (IRCA) and later revisions made it illegal for an employer to discriminate in recruiting, hiring, disciplining, or terminating employees based on an individual's national origin or citizenship. At the same time, the IRCA requires that employers who knowingly hire illegal aliens be penalized. Employers must ask for proof of identity, such as a driver's license with a picture, Social Security card, birth certificate, or immigration permit as part of completing the required I-9 form. This form must be completed by all new employees within 72 hours.

Other Types of Discrimination

Several other types of discrimination have been identified as illegal. A number of different types of discrimination require additional attention by employers.

Racial/Ethnic Harassment The area of racial/ethnic harassment is such a concern that the EEOC has issued guidelines on it. It is recommended that employers adopt policies against harassment of any type including ethnic jokes, vulgar epithets, racial slurs, and physical actions.

Religious Discrimination Title VII of the Civil Rights Act identifies discrimination on the basis of religion as illegal. However, religious schools and institutions can use religion as a bona fide occupational qualification for employment practices on a limited scale. Also, the employers must make *reasonable accommodation* efforts regarding an employee's religious beliefs.[8]

Genetic Bias Regulations Somewhat related to medical disabilities is the emerging area of workplace genetic bias. As medical research has revealed the human genome, medical tests have been developed that can identify an individual's genetic markers for various diseases. Whether these tests should be used and how they are used raise ethical issues.

Appearance and Weight Discrimination Several EEO cases have been filed concerning the physical appearance of employees. Court decisions consistently have allowed employers to set dress codes as long as they are applied uniformly. The crucial factor that employers must consider is that any weight or height requirements must be related to the job, such as when excess weight would hamper an individual's job performance.[9]

Sexual Orientation Recent battles in a number of states and communities illustrate the depth of emotions that accompany discussions of "gay rights." Some states and cities have passed laws prohibiting discrimination based on sexual orientation or lifestyle.

Military Status The employment rights of military veterans and reservists have been addressed in several laws. The two most important laws are the Vietnam Era Veterans Readjustment Assistance Act of 1974 and the Uniformed Services Employment and Reemployment Rights Act (USERRA) of 1994.

MANAGING DIVERSITY

As the foregoing discussion has indicated, the U.S. workforce has become quite diverse, and EEO regulation has encouraged and protected that diversity. Different organizations approach the management of diversity from several perspectives. The increasing diversity of the available workforce, combined with growing shortages of workers in many occupations and industries, has forced more employers to recognize that diversity must be managed.[10]

A wide variety of programs and activities have been used in organizations as part of diversity management efforts. Figure 3.4 shows common components of diversity management efforts. For diversity to succeed, the most crucial component is seeing it as a commitment throughout the organization, beginning with top management. Diversity results must be measured, and management accountability for

FIGURE 3.4 Common Diversity Management Components

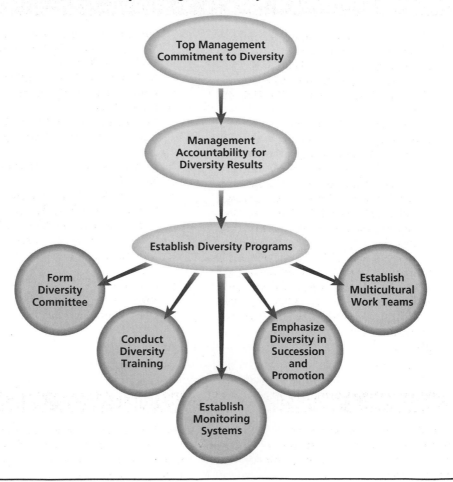

achieving these results must be emphasized and rewarded. Once management accountability for diversity results has been established, then a number of different activities can be implemented as part of a diversity management program, including diversity training. There are a number of different goals for traditional diversity training. One prevalent goal is to minimize discrimination and harassment lawsuits. Other goals focus on improving acceptance and understanding of people with different backgrounds, experiences, capabilities, and lifestyles.

The effects of diversity training are viewed as mixed by both organizations and participants. Relatively few studies have been done on the effectiveness of diversity training expenditures, other than asking participants how they felt about the training. There is some concern that the programs may be interesting or entertaining, but may not produce longer-term changes in people's attitudes and behaviors toward others with characteristics different from their own.[11]

NOTES

1. U.S. Equal Employment Opportunity Commission, "EEOC Reports Discrimination Charge Filings Up," February 6, 2003, *http://www.eeoc.gov/press/2-6-03.html.*
2. *Griggs v. Duke Power Co.,* 401 U.S. 424 (1971).
3. Harry Holzer and David Neumark, "What Does Affirmative Action Do?" *Industrial and Labor Relations Review,* 53 (2000), 240–271; Markus Kemmelmeier, "Individualism and Attitudes Toward Affirmative Action," *Basic and Applied Social Psychology,* 25 (2003), 111–119; T. J. Elkins et al., "Promotion Decisions in an Affirmative Action Environment," *Journal of Applied Social Psychology,* 33 (2003), 1111–1139; and Daniel Sabbagh, "Judicial Uses of Subterfuge: Affirmative Action Reconsidered," *Political Science Quarterly,* 118 (2003), 411–436.
4. "Sexual Orientation Irrelevant in Sex Harassment Claims," *HR News,* November 2002, 6.
5. Sue Shellenbarger, "Number of Woman Managers Rises," *Wall Street Journal,* September 30, 2003, D2.
6. Andy Meisler, "The Mindfield of Depression," *Workforce Management,* September 2003, 57–60.
7. "Implementation of the Employment Provisions of ADA/DDA," *http://www.shrm.org/global.*
8. TransWorld Airlines v. Hardison 432 U.S. 63 (1977).
9. Mark V. Roehling, "Weight Discrimination in the American Workplace," *Journal of Business Ethics,* 40 (2002), 177–189.
10. "Turn Diversity to Your Advantage," *Research Technology Management,* July 2003, 1–8.
11. C. W. Von Bergen et al., "Unintended Negative Effects of Diversity Management," *Public Personnel Management,* 31 (2002), 1–12.

INTERNET RESOURCES

Diversity, Inc. This site provides news, resources, and other commentary on the role of diversity in corporations. **http://www. diversityinc.com**

Equal Employment Advisory Council The EEAC is a nonprofit association of employers focused on equal employment opportunities. **http://www.eeac.org**

SUGGESTED READINGS

M. June Allard and Carol P. Harvey, *Understanding and Managing Diversity,* 2nd ed., Prentice-Hall, 2004

John F. Buckley, *Equal Employment Opportunity, Compliance Guide,* Aspen Publishing, 2005.

Lee Garderswartz and Anita Rowe, *Diverse Teams at Work,* Society for Human Resource Management, 2003.

William H. Truesdell, *Secrets of Affirmative Action Compliance,* Management Advantage, 2003.

Chapter 4

Staffing

The staffing process matches people with jobs through job analysis, recruiting, and selection. All three of these activities must be coordinated for employers to match organizational jobs with qualified applicants.

Managerial Perspectives on HR

1. How would you do a job analysis in a company that has never had job descriptions?
2. How could a bank use the Internet effectively to recruit management trainees?
3. How would you do a complete background investigation on applicants to minimize concerns about negligent hiring?

NATURE OF JOB ANALYSIS

Various methods and sources of data can be used to conduct job analyses. The real value of job analysis begins as the information is compiled into job descriptions and job specifications for use in virtually all HR activities. To justify HR actions as job related for EEO matters, accurate details on job requirements are needed. To be effective, HR planning, recruiting, and selection all must be based on job requirements and the capabilities of individuals. Additionally, compensation, training, and employee performance appraisals all should be based on the specific needs of the job. Job analysis also is useful in identifying job factors and duties that may contribute to workplace health and safety issues.

Job analysis involves collecting information on the characteristics of a job that differentiate it from other jobs. The information generated by job analysis may be useful in redesigning jobs, but its primary purpose is to capture a clear understanding of what is done on a job and what capabilities are needed to do it as designed. There are two approaches to job analysis, one focusing on tasks performed in the job, the other on competencies needed for job performance (Figure 4.1).

Task-Based Job Analysis

Task-based job analysis is the most common form and focuses on the tasks, duties, and responsibilities performed in a job. A **task** is a distinct, identifiable work activity composed of motions, whereas a **duty** is a larger work segment composed of several tasks that are performed by an individual. Because both tasks and duties

FIGURE 4.1 Job Analysis in Perspective

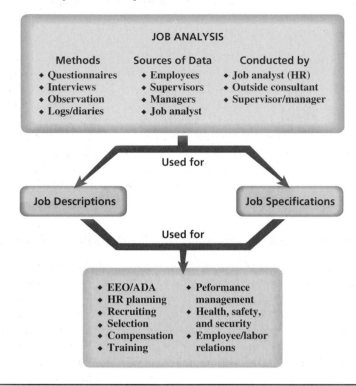

describe activities, it is not always easy or necessary to distinguish between the two. **Responsibilities** are obligations to perform certain tasks and duties.

Competency-Based Job Analysis

Unlike the traditional approach to analyzing jobs, which identifies the tasks, duties, knowledge, and skills associated with a job, the competency approach considers how the knowledge and skills are used. **Competencies** are individual capabilities that can be linked to enhanced performance by individuals or teams.

The concept of competencies varies widely from organization to organization. *Technical competencies* often refer to specific knowledge and skills employees have. For example, skills for using specialized software to design Web pages or for operating highly complex machinery and equipment may be cited as competencies. Some of the following have been identified as *behavioral competencies:*

- ► Customer focus
- ► Team orientation
- ► Technical expertise
- ► Results orientation
- ► Communication effectiveness

- ► Leadership
- ► Conflict resolution
- ► Innovation
- ► Adaptability
- ► Decisiveness

Whether to use the task-based or competency-based approach to job analysis is affected by the nature of jobs and how work is changing.

Conducting the Job Analysis

Once data from job analysis are compiled, the information should be sorted by job, organizational unit, and job family. This step allows for comparison of data from similar jobs throughout the organization. The data also should be reviewed for completeness, with follow-up as needed in the form of additional interviews or questions to be answered by managers and/or employees. Then the job analysts draft job descriptions and job specifications. Once job descriptions and specifications have been completed and reviewed by all appropriate individuals, a system must be developed for keeping them current. One effective way to ensure that appropriate reviews occur is to use job descriptions and job specifications in other HR activities.

Job Analysis and the Americans with Disabilities Act (ADA)

HR managers and their organizations must identify job activities and then document the steps taken to identify job responsibilities. One result of the ADA is increased emphasis by employers on conducting job analysis, as well as developing and maintaining current and accurate job descriptions and job specifications.

The ADA requires that organizations identify the **essential job functions,** which are the fundamental duties of a job. These do not include the marginal functions of the positions. **Marginal job functions** are duties that are part of a job but are incidental or ancillary to the purpose and nature of the job.

Job Analysis and Wage/Hour Regulations

Typically, job analysis identifies the percentage of time spent on each duty in a job. This information helps determine whether someone should be classified as exempt or nonexempt under the wage/hour laws.

The federal Fair Labor Standards Act (FLSA) and most state wage/hour laws indicate that the percentage of time employees spend on manual, routine, or clerical duties affects whether they must be paid overtime for hours worked in excess of 40 a week. To be exempt from overtime, the employees must perform their *primary duties* as executive, administrative, professional, or outside sales employees. *Primary* has been interpreted to mean occurring at least 50% of the time.

JOB DESCRIPTIONS AND JOB SPECIFICATIONS

The output from analysis of a job is used to develop a job description and its job specifications. Together, these summarize job analysis information in a readable format and provide the basis for defensible job-related actions. They also identify individual jobs for employees by providing documentation from management.

In most cases, the job description and job specifications are combined into one document that contains several sections. A **job description** identifies the tasks, duties, and responsibilities of a job. It describes what is done, why it is done, where it is done, and, briefly, how it is done. A typical job description contains several major parts. (See Appendix C for a sample of a job description.) **Performance standards** flow directly from a job description, and indicate what the job accomplishes and how performance is measured in key areas of the job description.

While the job description describes activities to be done, the **job specifications** list the knowledge, skills, and abilities (KSAs) an individual needs to perform a job satisfactorily. KSAs include education, experience, work skill requirements, personal abilities, and mental and physical requirements. It is important to note that accurate job specifications identify what KSAs a person needs to do the job, not necessarily the current employee's qualifications.

STRATEGIC APPROACH TO RECRUITING

The staffing process matches people with jobs through recruiting and selection. **Recruiting** is the process of generating a pool of qualified applicants for organizational jobs. If the number of available candidates only equals the number of people to be hired, no real selection is required—the choice has already been made. The organization must either leave some openings unfilled or take all the candidates.

A strategic approach to recruiting becomes more important as labor markets shift and become more competitive. Strategic HR planning helps to align HR strategies with organizational goals and plans. Therefore, it is important that recruiting be a part of strategic HR planning. For example, at one time, Walgreens, the drugstore chain, had to cut back its plans to expand and open new stores, because of a shortage of trained pharmacists. Good recruiting and more lead time might have kept it from having to do that and allowed the strategic expansion to go forward.

Labor Markets and Recruiting Decisions

Because staffing takes place in such variable labor markets, learning some basics about labor markets aids in understanding recruiting. **Labor markets** are the external supply pool from which employers attract employees. The supply of workers in various labor markets substantially affects staffing. An organization can recruit in a number of labor markets, including geographic, industry and occupational, and educational and technical. One common way to classify labor markets is based on geographic location. Some markets are local, some area or regional, some national, and others international. Local and area labor markets vary significantly in terms of workforce availability and quality.

An initial and basic decision is whether the recruiting will be done by the employer or outsourced. This decision need not be an "either-or" decision, with all recruiting done by organizational staff or else external resources used exclusively.

Because recruiting can be a time-consuming process, given all the other responsibilities of HR staff and other managers in organizations, outsourcing is a way to both decrease the number of HR staff needed and free up time for HR staff members.[1]

A specific type of outsourcing uses professional employer organizations (PEOs) and employee leasing. The employee leasing process is simple: An employer signs an agreement with the PEO, after which the existing staff is hired by the leasing firm and leased back to the company. For a fee, a small business owner or operator turns the staff over to the leasing company, which then writes the paychecks, pays the taxes, prepares and implements HR policies, and keeps all the required records.

Training of Recruiters

Another important strategic issue is how much training will be given to recruiters. In addition to being trained on interviewing techniques, communications skills, and knowledge of the jobs being filled, it is crucial that recruiters learn the types of actions that violate EEO regulations and how to be sensitive to diversity issues with applicants. Training in these areas often includes interview do's and don'ts and appropriate language to use with applicants.

Regular versus Flexible Staffing

Another strategic decision affects how much recruiting will be done to fill staffing needs with regular full-time and part-time employees. Decisions as to who should be recruited hinge on whether to seek traditional employees or to use more flexible approaches, which might include temporaries or independent contractors. A number of employers feel that the cost of keeping a regular workforce has become excessive and grows worse due to increasing government-mandated costs.

Flexible staffing uses workers who are not traditional employees. Using flexible staffing arrangements allows an employer to avoid some of the cost of full-time benefits such as vacation pay and pension plans, as well as to recruit in a somewhat different market. These arrangements provide temporary workers, independent contractors, and employee leasing.

INTERNAL RECRUITING

Recruiting strategy and policy decisions entail identifying where to recruit, whom to recruit, and how to recruit. One of the first decisions determines the extent to which internal or external sources and methods will be used. Both promoting from within the organization (internal recruitment) and hiring from outside the organization (external recruitment) come with advantages and disadvantages.

Within the organization, tapping into databases, job postings, promotions, and transfers provides ways for current employees to move to other jobs. Filling openings internally may add motivation for employees to stay and grow in the organization rather than pursuing career opportunities elsewhere.

Job Posting

The major means for recruiting employees for other jobs within the organization is **job posting,** a system in which the employer provides notices of job openings and employees respond by applying for specific openings. Without some sort of job posting system, it is difficult for many employees to find out what jobs are open elsewhere in the organization. The organization can notify employees of job vacancies in a number of ways, including posting notices on the company intranet and Internet Web site, using employee newsletters, and sending out e-mails to managers and employees.

Promotions and Transfers

Many organizations choose to fill vacancies through promotions or transfers from within whenever possible. Although most often successful, promotions and transfers from within have some drawbacks as well. A person's performance on one job may not be a good predictor of performance on another, because different skills may be required on the new job. For example, not every high-performing worker makes a successful supervisor. In most supervisory jobs, an ability to accomplish the work through others requires skills in influencing and dealing with people, and these skills may not have been a factor in nonsupervisory jobs.

Employee-Focused Recruiting

One reliable source of potential recruits is suggestions from current or former employees. Because current and former employees are familiar with the employer, most employees usually do not refer individuals who are likely to be unqualified or to make the employees look bad. Also, follow-up with former employees is likely to be done only with persons who were solid employees previously.

EXTERNAL RECRUITING SOURCES

There are a wide variety of external sources for recruiting. Some of the key ones are:

▶ *Colleges, universities and schools:* College or university students are a significant source for entry-level professional and technical employees. Most universities maintain career placement offices in which employers and applicants can meet. Also, high schools or vocational/technical schools may be good sources of new employees for some organizations.

▶ *Labor Unions:* Labor unions are a good source of certain types of workers. In such industries as electrical and construction ones, unions have traditionally supplied workers to employers. A labor pool is generally available through a union, and workers can be dispatched from it to particular jobs to meet the needs of the employers.

▶ *Employment Agencies:* Every state in the United States has its own state-sponsored employment agency. These agencies operate branch offices in many cities throughout the states and do not charge fees to applicants or employers. Private employment agencies also operate in most cities.

▶ *Competitive and Media Sources:* Other sources for recruiting include professional and trade associations, trade publications, and competitors. Such sources may be useful for recruiting specialized professionals needed in an industry. Media sources such as newspapers, magazines, television, radio, and billboards are widely used as well.

▶ *Job Fairs and Special Events:* Employers in tight labor markets or needing to fill a large number of jobs quickly have used job fairs and special recruiting events. Job fairs also have been held by economic development entities, employer associations, HR associations, and other community groups to help bring employers and potential job candidates together.[2]

INTERNET RECRUITING

The percentage of Global 500 companies that use Web sites for recruiting has jumped to 88%. Use of the Internet has increased around the globe in part because it is cheaper. The Internet is used for recruiting most widely in the United States: 12.2% of Internet users in the United States visited a Web site for recruitment in 2003, while only 7.3% of Internet users in Europe did so.[3] The explosive growth of Internet recruiting can overwhelm HR professionals in breadth and scope.

E-Recruiting Methods

Several methods are used for Internet recruiting. The most common ones are Internet job boards, professional/career Web sites, and employer Web sites.

Job boards provide access to numerous candidates. However, many individuals accessing the sites are "job lookers" who are not serious about changing jobs, but are checking out compensation levels and job availability in their areas of interest. Various estimates are that about one-third of all visitors to job boards are just browsing, not seriously considering changing employment.

Many professional associations have employment sections at their Web sites. As illustration, for HR jobs see the Society for Human Resource Management site, *http://www.shrm.org,* or the American Society for Training and Development site, *http://www.astd.org.*

Despite the popularity of job boards and association job sites, many employers have found their own Web sites to be more effective and efficient when recruiting candidates. Numerous employers have included employment and career information on their sites. According to one survey, about 16% of hires come through a company Web site—a much higher proportion than online job boards.[4]

Advantages and Disadvantages of Internet Recruiting

Employers have found a number of advantages in using Internet recruiting. A primary one is that many employers have saved money using Internet recruiting versus other recruiting methods such as newspaper advertising, employment agencies, and search firms.

Internet recruiting also can save considerable *time*. Applicants can respond quickly to job postings by sending e-mails, rather than using "snail mail." Recruiters can respond to qualified candidates more quickly, and establish times for interviews or request additional candidate information.

The positives associated with Internet recruiting come with a number of disadvantages. In getting broader exposure, employers also may get more unqualified applicants. HR recruiters find that Internet recruiting creates additional work for HR staff members. A related concern is that many individuals who access job sites are just browsers who may submit resumes just to see what happens but are not seriously looking for new jobs. Finally, with internet recruiting come new legal concerns.[5]

RECRUITING EVALUATION AND METRICS

As one means of evaluating recruiting, organizations can see how their recruiting efforts compare with past patterns and with the recruiting performance of other organizations. General metrics for evaluating quantity and quality of recruiting include the following variables:

▶ *Quantity of applicants:* Because the goal of a good recruiting program is to generate a large pool of applicants from which to choose, quantity is a natural place to begin evaluation. The basic measure here considers whether the quantity of recruits is sufficient to fill job vacancies.
▶ *Quality of applicants:* A key issue is whether or not the qualifications of the applicant pool are sufficient to fill the job openings. Do the applicants meet job specifications, and do they perform the jobs well after hire? What is the failure rate for new hires for each recruiter?
▶ *Time to fill:* Looking at the length of time it takes to fill openings is a common means of evaluating recruiting efforts. If openings are not filled quickly with qualified candidates, the work and productivity of the organization likely suffer.

Evaluating the Cost of Recruiting

The major number for measuring cost is calculating recruiting expenses for the year divided by the number of hires for the year:

Recruiting expenses/Number of recruits hired

The problem with this approach is accurately identifying what should be included in the recruiting expenses. Should expenses for testing, background checks, relocations, or signing bonuses be included, or are they more properly excluded?

Other metrics for measuring recruiting efforts include several, as follows:

▶ *Cost Benefit Analysis:* Because recruiting activities are important, the costs and benefits associated with them should be analyzed. A cost-benefit analysis of recruiting efforts may include both direct costs (advertising, recruiters' salaries, travel, agency fees, etc.) and indirect costs (involvement of operating managers, public relations, image, etc.).

▶ *Yield Ratios:* One means for evaluating recruiting efforts is **yield ratios,** which compare the number of applicants at one stage of the recruiting process with the number at another stage. The result is a tool for approximating the necessary size of the initial applicant pool.

▶ *Selection Rate:* Another useful calculation is the **selection rate,** which is the percentage hired from a given group of candidates. It equals the number hired divided by the number of applicants; for example, a rate of 30% indicates that 3 out of 10 applicants were hired. The selection rate is also affected by the validity of the selection process.

SELECTION AND PLACEMENT

Selection decisions are an important part of successful HR management. Perhaps the best perspective on selection and placement comes from two HR truisms that clearly identify the importance of an effective selection process:

▶ *Hire hard, manage easy:* The amount of time and effort spent selecting the right people for jobs may make managing them as employees much less difficult because more problems will be eliminated.

▶ *Good training will not make up for bad selection:* When the right people with the appropriate capabilities are not selected for jobs, employers have difficulty later adequately training those individuals who are selected.

The ultimate purpose of selection is **placement** or fitting a person to the right job. Placement of human resources should be seen as primarily a matching process. Selection and placement activities typically focus on applicant's knowledge, skills, and abilities. The **person/job fit** is a simple but important concept that involves matching the KSAs of people with the characteristics of jobs. People already in jobs can help identify the most important KSAs for success, as part of job analysis.

Criteria, Predictors, and Job Performance

Whether an employer uses specific KSAs or a more general approach, effective selection of employees involves using criteria and predictors of job performance. At the heart of an effective selection system must be knowledge of what constitutes appropriate job performance and what employee characteristics are associated with that performance. First, an employer defines successful employee performance; then, using that definition as a basis, the employer determines the employee KSAs required to achieve that success. A **selection criterion** is a characteristic that a person must have to do a specific job successfully. Figure 4.2 shows that ability, motivation, intelligence, conscientiousness, appropriate risk, and permanence might be good selection criteria for many jobs.

FIGURE 4.2 Job Performance, Selection Criteria, and Predictors

To determine whether or not candidates might have a certain selection criterion (such as ability or motivation), employers try to identify **predictors** that are measurable or visible indicators—of that criterion. For example, in Figure 4.2, three good predictors of permanence might be individual interests, salary requirements, and tenure on previous jobs.

The information gathered about an applicant through predictors should be focused on the likelihood that the applicant will be able to perform the job well. Predictors can take many forms (for example, application form, test, interview, education requirements, or years of experience required), but they should be used only if they are valid predictors of job performance. Using invalid predictors can result in selecting the "wrong" candidate and rejecting the "right" one.

Validity In selection, validity is the correlation between a predictor and job performance. Validity occurs to the extent that a predictor actually predicts what it is supposed to predict. Validity depends on the situation in which the selection device is being used. For example, a psychological test designed to predict aptitude for child-care jobs might not be valid in predicting sales aptitude for marketing representative jobs. Clearly, if a test is not valid, it should not be used. A test must be validated for use in a specific company's application, not "in general" by the test vendor.

Reliability Reliability of a predictor is the extent to which it repeatedly produces the same results, over time. For example, if a person took a test in December and scored 75, then took it again in March and scored significantly lower, the test may not be reliable. Thus, reliability has to do with the consistency of predictors used in selection.

THE SELECTION PROCESS

Most organizations take a series of consistent steps to process and select applicants for jobs. Variations on the basic process depend on organizational size, nature of the jobs to be filled, number of people to be selected, the use of electronic technology, and other factors. This process can take place in a day or over a much longer period of time. If the applicant is processed in one day, the employer usually checks references after selection. One or more phases of the process may be omitted or the order changed, depending on the employer. Figure 4.3 shows parts of the selection process.

Applicant Job Interest

Individuals desiring employment can indicate interest in a number of ways. Traditionally, individuals have submitted resumes by mail or fax, or applied in person at an employer's location. But with the growth in Internet recruiting, many individuals complete applications online or submit resumes electronically.

Most job seekers appear to know little about organizations before applying to them for jobs. Through the process of a **realistic job preview (RJP),** applicants are provided with an accurate picture of a job, including the "organizational realities" surrounding it, so that they can better evaluate their own job expectations. With an RJP, the organization hopes to prevent unrealistic expectations, which helps reduce employee disenchantment and ultimately employee dissatisfaction and turnover.

Pre-employment Screening

Many employers conduct preemployment screening to determine if applicants meet the minimum qualifications for open jobs. Because these minimum standards are required, it would be a waste of time for any applicant who could not meet them to fill out an application form initially. Some areas typically covered by employers include types of available jobs, applicants' pay expectations, job location, and travel requirements.

Application Forms

Application forms are almost universally used and can take different formats. Properly prepared, the application form serves four purposes:

▶ It is a record of the applicant's desire to obtain a position.
▶ It provides the interviewer with a profile of the applicant that can be used in the interview.

FIGURE 4.3 Selection Process Flowchart

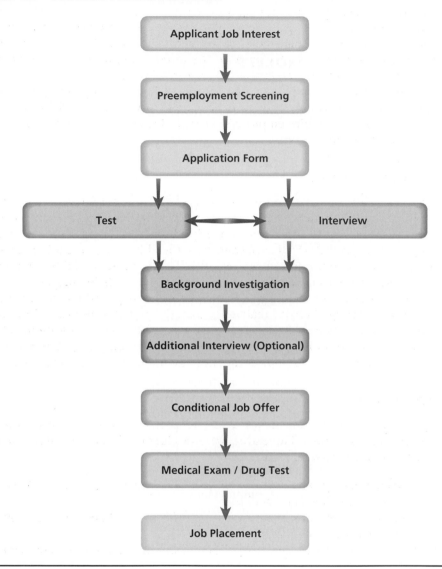

- ▶ It is a basic employee record for applicants who are hired.
- ▶ It can be used for research on the effectiveness of the selection process.

Many employers use only one application form, but others need several. For example, a hospital might need one form for nurses and medical technicians, another form for clerical and office employees, another for managers and supervisors, and yet another for support workers in housekeeping and food-service areas.

Immigration Forms

The Immigration Reform and Control Act of 1986, as revised in 1990, requires that within 72 hours of hiring, an employer must determine whether a job applicant is a U.S. citizen, registered alien, or illegal alien. Applicants who are not eligible to work in this country must not be hired. Employers use the I-9 form to identify the status of potential employees. Employers are responsible for ensuring the legitimacy of documents submitted by new employees, such as U.S. passports, birth certificates, original Social Security cards, and driver's licenses. Also, employers who hire employees on special visas must maintain appropriate documentation and records.

Selection Testing

Many kinds of tests may be used to help select good employees. Literacy tests, skills tests, psychological measurement tests, and honesty tests are the major categories. Carefully developed and properly administered employment tests allow employers to predict which applicants have the ability to do the job in question, who can learn in training, and who will stay. Tests are even available to screen out candidates who may create behavioral or other risks to the employer.[6]

A recent survey found that 41% of the employers polled use basic skills tests (essentially testing ability to read and do math) and 68% use some kind of job skills test (focusing on skills necessary to do a specific job). In addition, 29% use some kind of psychological measurement test (including cognitive ability, personality, and honesty).[7] A look at the most common types of tests follows.

Ability Tests

Tests that assess an individual's ability to perform in a specific manner are grouped as ability tests. These are sometimes further differentiated into *aptitude tests* and *achievement tests,* as follows:

▶ **Cognitive ability tests** measure an individual's thinking, memory, reasoning, verbal, and mathematical abilities.
▶ **Physical ability tests** measure an individual's abilities such as strength, endurance, and muscular movement.
▶ **Work sample tests** require an applicant to perform a simulated task that is part of the target job.
▶ **Situational judgment tests** are designed to measure a person's judgment in work settings. The candidate is given a situation and a list of possible solutions to the problem.

Personality Tests

Personality is a unique blend of individual characteristics that affect interaction with a person's environment and help define a person. Many types of personality tests are available. One well-known version is the Minnesota Multiphasic Personality Inventory (MMPI), which was originally developed to diagnose major psychological disorders and has become widely used as a selection test. The Myers-Briggs test is another widely used instrument of the same type. From these and many other personality tests, an extensive number of personality characteristics can be identified and used. When used in selection, psychological or personality testing must be solidly related to the job.

Honesty/Integrity Tests

Different types of tests are being used by employers to assess the honesty and integrity of applicants and employees. They include standardized honesty/integrity tests and polygraph tests. Both are controversial. However, it is important that the tests be chosen, used, and evaluated in ways that ensure that they are and remain valid and reliable.

SELECTION INTERVIEWING

Selection interviewing of job applicants is done both to obtain additional information and to clarify information gathered throughout the selection process. Typically, interviews are conducted at two levels: first, as an initial screening interview simply to see if the person has minimum qualifications, and then later, as an in-depth interview perhaps involving HR staff members and operating managers in the departments where the individuals will work.

Structured Interviews

A **structured interview** uses a set of standardized questions asked of all applicants. The interviewer asks every applicant the same basic questions, so that comparisons among applicants can more easily be made. This type of interview allows an interviewer to prepare job-related questions in advance and then complete a standardized interviewee evaluation form that provides documentation indicating why one applicant was selected over another.

Less-Structured Interviews

Some interviews are done unplanned and without any structure. Often, these interviews are conducted by operating managers or supervisors who have had little training on interviewing do's and don'ts. An *unstructured interview* occurs when the interviewer "wings it," asking questions that have no identified direct purpose, such as, "Tell me about yourself."

Problems in the Interview

Operating managers and supervisors are more likely to use poor interviewing techniques because they do not interview often or lack training. Several problems are commonly encountered in the interview.

Snap Judgments Unfortunately, many interviewers decide whether an applicant is suitable for the job within the first two to four minutes of the interview, and spend the balance of the interview looking for evidence to support their decision. This impression may be based on a review of the individual's application form or on more subjective factors such as dress or appearance. Ideally, the interviewer should collect all the information possible on an applicant before making a judgment.

Negative Emphasis As might be expected, unfavorable information about an applicant is the biggest factor considered in interviewers' decisions about overall suitability. Unfavorable information is usually given more weight than favorable information. Often, a single negative characteristic may bar an individual from being accepted, whereas no amount of positive characteristics will guarantee a candidate's acceptance.

Halo Effect Interviewers should try to avoid the *halo effect,* which occurs when an interviewer allows a prominent characteristic to overshadow other evidence. For instance, the halo effect is present if an interviewer lets a candidate's athletic accomplishments overshadow other characteristics, and then hires the applicant because "athletes make good salespeople." The term *Devil's horns* is the reverse of the term halo effect. It occurs when an interviewer allows a negative characteristic, such as inappropriate dress or a low grade point average, to overshadow other evidence.

Biases and Stereotyping Personal biases and stereotyping of applicants should be avoided in interviews. One type of bias, the "similarity" bias, occurs because interviewers tend to favor or select people they perceive to be similar to themselves. The similarity can be in age, race, sex, previous work experiences, personal background, or other factors. As workforce demographics shift, interviewers should be aware of any personal tendencies to stereotype individuals because of demographic characteristics and differences, and be careful to avoid doing so.

Cultural Noise Interviewers must learn to recognize and handle cultural noise, which comes from what the applicant believes is socially acceptable rather than what the applicant knows is factual. An interviewer can handle cultural noise by not encouraging it. If the interviewer supports cultural noise, the applicant will take the cue and continue giving answers that reflect it. If the interviewer instead makes the applicant aware that he or she is not being taken in, the interviewer reestablishes control over the interview. See Appendix D, "Effective Interviewing," for further discussion.

BACKGROUND INVESTIGATION

Background investigation may take place either before or after the in-depth interview. It costs the organization some time and money, but it generally proves beneficial when making selection decisions. Technology has played an increasing role in helping employers conduct background investigations.

A background screening has four goals: to show that the employer exercised due diligence in hiring; to provide factual information about a candidate; to discourage applicants with something to hide; to encourage applicants to be honest on applications and during interviews.

A comprehensive background check costs $100–$200 per applicant.[8] A few states have passed laws enforcing limitations on background checking that have made the process more complex, and have encouraged employers to hire firms that specialize in checking backgrounds. International background checks present special challenges. A common but dangerous assumption is that if an applicant has a visa, she or he is a safe choice for employment.

Sources of Background Information

Background information can be obtained from a number of sources. Personal references, such as those from relatives, clergy, or friends, are of little value, and should not even be used. No applicant seeks a recommendation from somebody who would give a negative response. Instead, work-related references from previous employers and supervisors should be relied on.

SHRM reports that the conducting of a criminal background check has increased by 29% in the last several years. Eighty percent of HR professionals say they conduct criminal checks, and 88% conduct some kind of background checks.[9] These checks reveal that 13% of those screened had failed to disclose a criminal background and 23% had misrepresented employment or education.[10]

Several methods of obtaining information from references are available to an employer, with telephoning the reference the most commonly used method. Many experts recommend that employers conducting a telephone reference check use a form focusing on factual verification of information given by the applicant, such as employment dates, salary history, type of job responsibilities, and attendance record. Other items often include reasons for leaving the previous job, the individual's manner of working with supervisors and other employees, and other more subjective information. Many firms that are called for references will provide only factual information. But the use of the form can provide evidence that a diligent effort was made.

MAKING THE JOB OFFER

The final step of the selection process is offering someone employment. Job offers are often extended over the phone, and many are then formalized in letters and sent to applicants. It is important that the offer document be reviewed by legal counsel and that the terms and conditions of employment be clearly identified. Care should be taken to avoid vague, general statements and promises about bonuses, work schedules, or other matters that might change later. These documents also should provide for the individuals to sign an acceptance of the offer and return it to the employer, who should place it in the individual's personnel files.

NOTES

1. Michelle Martinez, "Recruiting Here and There," *HR Magazine,* September 2002, 96–97.
2. Martha Frase-Blunt, "Job Fair Challenges for HR," *HR Magazine,* April 2002, 1–5.
3. Anne Freedman, "The Web World-Wide," *Human Resource Executive,* March 6, 2002, 44–46.
4. Karen Frankola, "Better Recruiting on Corporate Web Sites," *Workforce Online,* May 2002, *http://www.workforce.com.*
5. Gillian Flynn, "E-Recruiting Ushers in Legal Dangers," *Workforce,* April 2002, 70–72.
6. David Arnold and John Jones, "Who the Devil's Applying Now? Companies Can Use Tests to Screen Out Dangerous Job Candidates," *Security Management,* March 2002, 85.
7. "2001 AMA Survey on Workplace Testing," *AMA Research, http://www.amanet.org/research.*
8. Carroll Lachnit, "Protecting People and Profits with Background Checks," *Workforce,* February 2002, 50–54.
9. "SHRM Finds Employers Are Increasingly Conducting Background Checks to Ensure Workplace Safety," January 20, 2004, *http://www.shrm.org/press.*
10. Merry Mayer, "Background Checks in Focus," *HR Magazine,* January 2002, 1–4.

INTERNET RESOURCES

The Employment Strategist This Web site offers a free monthly newsletter focusing on the recruitment, selection, and retention of human resources in today's changing workforce. **http://www.cathyfyock.com**

Job Web This Web site offers a job outlook section containing a special report about labor markets and jobs. Also, it contains information on career fairs, starting salaries, and researching potential employers. **http://www.jobweb.com**

SUGGESTED READINGS

Michael T. Brannick and Edward L. Levine, *Job Analysis,* Corwin Press, 2002.

Michael Foster, *Recruiting on the Web,* McGraw-Hill, 2003

Barry Siegel, *Keys to Successful Recruiting and Staffing,* Weddle Publishing, 2003.

Aggie White, *Interview Styles and Strategies,* South-Western Educational Publishers, 2003.

Chapter 5

Training and Developing Human Resources

Managerial Perspectives on HR

1. What steps can HR professionals take to overcome the organizational tendency to cut training when money is tight?

2. How does development differ from training and why are both important to organizational performance?

3. Why is succession planning important in organizations of all sizes today?

The competitive pressures facing organizations today require employees whose knowledge and ideas are current, and whose skills and abilities can deliver results. As organizations compete and change, training becomes even more critical than before. Employees who must adapt to the many changes facing organizations must be trained and developed continually in order to maintain and update their capabilities. Also, managers must have training and development to enhance their leadership skills and abilities.

NATURE OF TRAINING

Training is the process whereby people acquire capabilities to perform jobs. Poorly trained employees may perform poorly and make costly mistakes. Training provides employees with specific, identifiable knowledge and skills for use in their present jobs. Sometimes a distinction is drawn between *training* and *development,* with development being broader in scope and focusing on individuals' gaining new capabilities useful for both present and future jobs.

Organizational Competitiveness and Training

More employers are recognizing that training their human resources is vital. Currently, U.S. employers spend at least $60 billion annually on training. For the average employer, training expenditures average at least 1.5%–2% of payroll expenses, and run $677 per eligible employee, according to a study by the American Society for Training and Development (ASTD). Organizations that see training as especially crucial to business competitiveness average $1,665 in training expenditures per eligible employee.[1]

Training also assists organizational competitiveness by aiding in the retention of employees. Employers that invest in training and developing their employees enhance retention efforts.

Knowledge management is the way an organization identifies and leverages knowledge in order to be competitive. Multiple definitions of knowledge management exist, some referring to the technology used to transfer information. Technology can indeed help transmit knowledge, but having technology does not mean people will use it to manage knowledge to best effect. Knowledge management is a conscious effort to get the right knowledge to the right people at the right time so that it can be shared and put into action. It involves more than simply a technological infrastructure.[2]

Performance Consulting

Training should result in improved organizational performance. Ensuring that it does may require a "performance consulting" approach. **Performance consulting** is a process in which a trainer (either internal or external to the organization) and the organizational client work together to decide what needs to be done to improve results. That may or may not include training.

Performance consulting compares desired and actual organizational results with desired and actual employee performance. Once these comparisons are made, then performance consulting takes a broad approach to performance issues.

Training and Organizational Strategy

Training represents a significant expenditure in most organizations. But it is too often viewed tactically rather than strategically, as upper management is often not clear what it wants from training and therefore fails to connect training with the strategy and goals of the organization. Figure 5.1 shows how training might be used to help accomplish various strategies in an organization. Ideally, the upper management group understands that the training function can provide valuable intelligence about the necessary core skills. If the training unit understands the strategic direction of the organization, it can find creative ways to move people in the direction of the various strategies.

FIGURE 5.1   Linking Organizational Strategies and Training

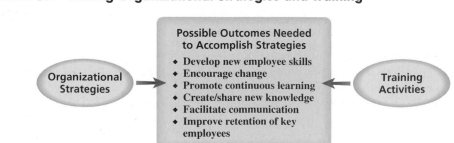

Training plans allow organizations to identify what is needed for employee performance *before* training begins. It is at this stage that fit with strategic issues is ensured. A good training plan deals with the following questions:[3]

▶ Is there really a need for the training?
▶ Who needs to be trained?
▶ Who will do the training?
▶ What form will the training take?
▶ How will knowledge be transferred to the job?
▶ How will the training be evaluated?

TRAINING PROCESS

The way firms organize and structure the training affects the way employees experience the training, which in turn influences the effectiveness of the training. Effective training requires the use of a systematic training process with four phases: assessment, design, delivery, and evaluation. Using such a process reduces the likelihood that unplanned, uncoordinated, and haphazard training efforts will occur. A discussion of each phase of the training process follows.

Training Needs Assessment

Assessing organizational training needs represents the diagnostic phase of a training plan. This assessment considers issues of employee and organizational performance to determine if training can help. Needs assessment measures the competencies of a company, a group, or an individual as they relate to what is required in the strategic plan. It is necessary to find out what is happening and what should be happening before deciding if training will help, and if it will help, what kind is needed.[4]

Establishing Training Objectives and Priorities

Once training needs have been identified using appropriate analyses, then training objectives and priorities can be established by a "gap analysis," which indicates the distance between where an organization is with its employee capabilities and where it needs to be. Training objectives and priorities are set to close the gap. Three types of training objectives can be set:

▶ *Knowledge:* Impart cognitive information and details to trainees.
▶ *Skill:* Develop behavior changes in how jobs and various task requirements are performed.
▶ *Attitude:* Create interest in and awareness of the importance of training.

The success of training should be measured in terms of the objectives set. Useful objectives are measurable. For example, an objective for a new sales clerk might be to "demonstrate the ability to explain the function of each product in the department within two weeks." This objective checks on internalization, or whether the person really learned and is able to use the training.

Training Design

Once training objectives have been determined, training design can start. Whether job-specific or broader in nature, training must be designed to address the assessed specific needs. Effective training design considers learning concepts, different approaches to training, and legal issues.

Learning Focus of Training   For training to be successful, learners must be ready to learn. Learner readiness means having the basic skills necessary for learning, the motivation to learn, and self-efficacy, or a person's belief that he or she can successfully learn the training program content. For learners to be ready for and receptive to the training content, they must feel that it is possible for them to learn it.

Learning Styles   In designing training interventions, trainers also should consider individual learning styles. For example, auditory learners learn best by listening to someone else tell them about the training content. Tactile learners must "get their hands on" the training resources and use them. Visual learners think in pictures and figures and need to sce the purpose and process of the training. Trainers who address all these styles by using multiple training methods can design more effective training.

Training many different people from diverse backgrounds poses a significant challenge in today's work organizations. Five principles for designing training for adults and subsequent work by others suggest that adults:

1.   Have the need to know why they are learning something
2.   Have a need to be self-directed
3.   Bring more work-related experiences into the learning process
4.   Enter into a learning experience with a problem-centered approach to learning
5.   Are motivated to learn by both extrinsic and intrinsic factors

Adult learners should be encouraged to bring work-related problems to training as a way to make the material more relevant to them.[5] Effective training should involve participants in learning by actively engaging them in the learning and problem-solving process.

The most elementary way in which people learn—and one of the best—is **behavior modeling,** or copying someone else's behavior. The use of behavior modeling is particularly appropriate for skill training in which the trainees must use both knowledge and practice.

Reinforcement and Immediate Confirmation   The concept of **reinforcement** is based on the *law of effect,* which states that people tend to repeat responses that give them some type of positive reward and to avoid actions associated with negative consequences. Closely related is a learning concept called **immediate confirmation,** which is based on the idea that people learn best if reinforcement and feedback are given as soon as possible after training. Immediate confirmation corrects errors that, if made throughout the training, might establish an undesirable pattern that would need to be unlearned. It also aids with the transfer of training to the actual work done.

Transfer of Training

Finally, trainers should design training for the highest possible transfer from the class to the job. Transfer occurs when trainees actually use on the job what they learned in training.

Effective transfer of training meets two conditions. First, the trainees can take the material learned in training and apply it to the job context in which they work. Second, employees maintain their use of the learned material over time. For example, training managers to be better selection interviewers should include role-playing with "applicants" who respond in the same way that real applicants would.

TRAINING CATEGORIES

Training can be designed to meet a number of objectives and can be classified in various ways. Some common groupings include the following:

- ▶ *Required and regular training:* Complies with various mandated legal requirements (e.g., OSHA and EEO) and is given to all employees (new employee orientation)
- ▶ *Job/technical training:* Enables employees to perform their jobs, tasks, and responsibilities well (e.g., product knowledge, technical processes and procedures, and customer relations)
- ▶ *Interpersonal and problem-solving training:* Addresses both operational and interpersonal problems and seeks to improve organizational working relationships (e.g., interpersonal communication, managerial/supervisory skills, and conflict resolution)
- ▶ *Developmental and innovative training:* Provides long-term focus to enhance individual and organizational capabilities for the future (e.g., business practices, executive development, and organizational change)

The most important and widely conducted type of regular training is done for *new* employees. **Orientation** is the planned introduction of new employees to their jobs, coworkers, and the organization, and is offered by most employers. It requires cooperation between individuals in the HR unit and operating managers and supervisors. In a small organization without an HR department, the new employee's supervisor or manager usually assumes most of the responsibility for orientation. In large organizations, managers and supervisors, as well as the HR department, generally work as a team to orient new employees.

Cross training occurs when people are trained to do more than one job—theirs and someone else's. For the employer, the advantages of cross training are flexibility and development. If an employee gets sick or quits, there is someone already trained to do the job. However, while cross training is attractive to the employer, it is not always appreciated by employees, who often feel that it requires them to do more work for the same pay.

TRAINING DELIVERY

Once training has been designed, then the actual delivery of training can begin. It is generally recommended that the training be pilot-tested or conducted on a trial basis to ensure that the training meets the needs identified and that the design is appropriate. Regardless of the type of training done, a number of approaches and methods can be used to deliver it. The growth of training technology continues to expand the available choices.

Internal Training

Internal training generally applies very specifically to a job. It is popular because it saves the cost of sending employees away for training and often avoids the cost of outside trainers.

One internal source of training is **informal training,** which occurs through interactions and feedback among employees. Much of what the employees know about their jobs they learn informally from asking questions and getting advice from other employees and their supervisors, rather than from formal training programs.

On-the-Job Training (OJT)   The most common type of training at all levels in an organization is *on-the-job training (OJT)*.[6] In contrast with informal training, which often occurs spontaneously, OJT should be planned. The supervisor or manager conducting the training must be able to both teach and show the employees what to do. Based on a guided form of training known as *job instruction training (JIT)*, on-the-job training is most effective if a logical progression of stages is used, as shown in Figure 5.2.

External Training

External training, or training that takes place outside the employing organization, is used extensively by organizations of all sizes. Whatever the size of the organization, external training occurs because:

▶ It may be less expensive for an employer to have an outside trainer conduct training in areas where internal training resources are limited.
▶ The organization may have insufficient time to develop internal training materials.

Outsourcing of Training   Many employers of all sizes outsource training to external training firms, consultants, and other entities. According to data from ASTD, approximately 28% of training expenditures go to outside training sources. Interestingly, over a recent three-year period, the outsourcing of training saw a

FIGURE 5.2   Stages for On-the-Job Training (OJT)

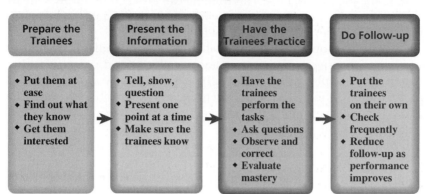

Prepare the Trainees	Present the Information	Have the Trainees Practice	Do Follow-up
• Put them at ease • Find out what they know • Get them interested	• Tell, show, question • Present one point at a time • Make sure the trainees know	• Have the trainees perform the tasks • Ask questions • Observe and correct • Evaluate mastery	• Put the trainees on their own • Check frequently • Reduce follow-up as performance improves

decline.[7] The reasons for the decline may be cost concerns, a greater emphasis on internal linking of training to organizational strategies, and other issues.

Educational Assistance Programs Some employers pay for additional education for their employees. Typically, the employee pays for courses that apply to a college degree and is reimbursed upon successful completion of a course. The amounts paid by the employer are considered nontaxable income for the employee up to amounts set by federal laws.

E-learning: Online Training

E-learning is use of the Internet or an organizational intranet to conduct training online. The rapid growth of e-learning makes the Internet or an intranet a viable means for delivering training content. E-learning has both advantages and disadvantages that must be considered. In addition to being concerned about employee access to e-learning and desire to use it, some employers worry that trainees will use e-learning to complete courses quickly but will not retain and use much of their learning.

In sum, e-learning is the latest development in the evolution of training delivery. Some of the biggest obstacles to using it will continue to be keeping up with the rapid change in technological innovation, knowing when and how much to invest, and designing e-courses appropriately.

Training Approaches

Whether training is delivered internally, externally, or through e-learning, appropriate training approaches must be chosen. Some are used more for job-based training, while others are used more for development.

Cooperative Training Cooperative training approaches mix classroom training and on-the-job experiences. This training can take several forms. One form, generally referred to as *school-to-work transition,* helps individuals move into jobs while still in school or upon completion of formal schooling.

A form of cooperative training called *internship* usually combines job training with classroom instruction from schools, colleges, and universities. Internships benefit both employers and interns. Interns get "real-world" exposure, a line on their resumes, and a chance to closely examine a possible employer. Employers get a cost-effective source of labor and a chance to see an intern at work before making a final hiring decision.

Another form of cooperative training used by employers, trade unions, and government agencies is *apprentice training.* An apprenticeship program provides an employee with on-the-job experience under the guidance of a skilled and certified worker.

Instructor-Led Classroom and Conference Training Instructor-led training is still the most prevalent approach to training. Employer-conducted short courses, lectures, and meetings usually consist of classroom training, whereas numerous employee development courses offered by professional organizations, trade associations, and educational institutions are examples of conference training.

Distance Training/Learning A growing number of college and university classes use some form of Internet-based course support. Blackboard and WebCT are two popular support packages that thousands of college professors use to make their lecture content available to students. These packages enable virtual chat and electronic file exchange among course participants, and also enhance instructor/student contact.

Simulations and Training The explosive growth in information technology in the past few years has revolutionized the way all individuals work, including how they are trained. Today, computer-based training involves a wide array of multimedia technologies—including sound, motion (video and animation), graphics, and hypertext—to tap multiple learner senses. Video streaming allows video clips of training materials to be stored on a firm's network server. Employees can then access the material using the firm's intranet.

TRAINING EVALUATION

Evaluation of training compares the posttraining results to the pretraining objectives of managers, trainers, and trainees. Too often, training is conducted with little thought of measuring and evaluating it later to see how well it worked. Because training is both time-consuming and costly, it should be evaluated.

Levels of Evaluation

It is best to consider how training is to be evaluated before it begins. Donald L. Kirkpatrick identified four levels at which training can be evaluated. As Figure 5.3

FIGURE 5.3   Levels of Training Evaluation

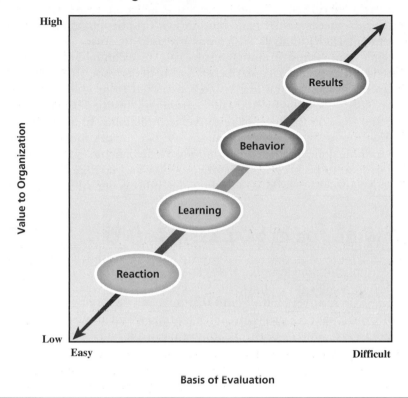

shows, the evaluation of training becomes successively more difficult as it moves from measuring reaction, to measuring learning, to measuring behavior, and then to measuring results. But the training that affects behavior and results versus reaction and learning provides greater value.

Reaction   Organizations evaluate the reaction levels of trainees by conducting interviews with or administering questionnaires to the trainees.

Learning   Learning levels can be evaluated by measuring how well trainees have learned facts, ideas, concepts, theories, and attitudes.

Behavior   Evaluating training at the behavioral level means: (1) measuring the effect of training on job performance through interviews of trainees and their coworkers and (2) observing job performance.

Results   Employers evaluate results by measuring the effect of training on the achievement of organizational objectives. Because results such as productivity, turnover, quality, time, sales, and costs are relatively concrete, this type of evaluation can be done by comparing records before and after training.

Training Evaluation Metrics

As mentioned earlier, training is expensive, and therefore it is one HR function that requires measurement and monitoring. Cost-benefit analysis and return-on-investment (ROI) analysis are commonly used to do so, as are various benchmarking approaches. Training results can be examined through **cost-benefit analysis,** which is comparison of costs and benefits associated with training.

In organizations, training is often expected to produce a return-on-investment. Still, in too many circumstances, training is justified because someone liked it, rather than on the basis of resource accountability. In addition to evaluating training internally, some organizations use benchmark measures to compare it with training done in other organizations. To do benchmarking, HR professionals gather data on training in their organization and compare them with data on training at other organizations in the same industry and of a similar size.

TRAINING FOR GLOBAL ASSIGNMENTS

The orientation and training that expatriates and their families receive before departure significantly affect the success of an overseas assignment. Unfortunately, various surveys have found that only 50%–60% of global employers provide formal training programs for expatriates and their families. When such programs are offered, most expatriates participate in them, and the programs usually produce a positive effect on cross-cultural adjustment.[8]

Growing numbers of global employers are providing intercultural competence training for their global employees. Intercultural competence incorporates a wide range of human social skills and personality characteristics. The key components are:

▶ *Cognitive:* What does the person know about other cultures?
▶ *Emotional:* How does the person view other cultures, and how sensitive is the person to cultural customs and issues?
▶ *Behavioral:* How does the person act in intercultural situations?

Transfers and promotions offer opportunities for employees to develop. However, unlike new hires, employees who have moved to new positions are often expected to perform well immediately, though that may not be realistic. International transfers cause even more difficulties than in-country transfers for many.

CAREERS AND CAREER PLANNING

A **career** is the series of work-related positions a person occupies throughout life. People pursue careers to satisfy deeply individual needs. At one time, identifying with one employer seemed to fulfill many of those needs. Now, individuals and organizations view careers in distinctly different ways.

Rather than letting jobs define their lives, more people set goals for the type of lives they want and then use jobs to meet those goals. However, for dual-career couples and working women, balancing work demands with personal and family responsibilities is a growing challenge.

For employers, career issues have changed too. The best people will not go to workplaces viewed as undesirable, because they do not have to do so. Employers must focus on retaining and developing talented workers by providing coaching, mentoring, and appropriate assignments.

Career Planning Perspectives

Effective career planning considers both organization-centered and individual-centered perspectives. Figure 5.4 summarizes the perspectives and interaction between the organizational and individual approaches to career planning. The next section takes a look at both these approaches.

Organization-Centered Career Planning

Organization-centered career planning focuses on identifying career paths that provide for the logical progression of people between jobs in an organization. Individuals follow these paths as they advance in organizational units.

The systems an employer uses to manage careers in the organization should be planned and managed in an integrated fashion to guide managers in developing employees' careers. One such system is the career path, or "map," which is created and shared with the individual employee.

Organizational retrenchment and downsizing have changed career plans for many people. More and more individuals have had to face "career transitions"—in other words, they have had to find new jobs. These transitions have identified the importance of individual-centered career planning.

FIGURE 5.4   Organizational and Individual Career Planning Perspectives

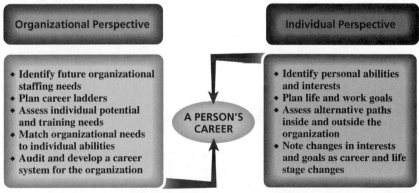

Organizational Perspective

- Identify future organizational staffing needs
- Plan career ladders
- Assess individual potential and training needs
- Match organizational needs to individual abilities
- Audit and develop a career system for the organization

A PERSON'S CAREER

Individual Perspective

- Identify personal abilities and interests
- Plan life and work goals
- Assess alternative paths inside and outside the organization
- Note changes in interests and goals as career and life stage changes

Individual-centered career planning focuses on an individual's career rather than on organizational needs. It is done by the employees themselves when they analyze their individual goals and capabilities. Such efforts might consider situations both inside and outside the organization that could expand a person's career.

Because individual-centered career planning focuses on the individual, it may change depending on shifts in the individual's interests, abilities, circumstances, and family issues. For individuals today, careers are rarely lived out in a single organizational setting. Instead, careers are "boundaryless" in that they might span several companies, industries, jobs, and projects.

Career Transitions and HR

Three career transitions are of special interests to HR: organizational entry and socialization, transfers and promotions, and job loss. Starting as a new employee can be overwhelming. "Entry shock" is especially difficult for younger new hires who find the work world very different from school.

Transfers and promotions offer opportunities for employees to develop. However, unlike new hires, employees who have moved to new positions are often expected to perform well immediately, though that may not be realistic. International transfers cause even more difficulties than in-country transfers for many.

Job loss has been most associated with downsizing, mergers, and acquisitions. Losing a job is a stressful event in one's career, frequently causing depression, anxiety, and nervousness. The financial implications and the effects on family can be extreme as well. Yet the potential for job loss continues to increase and should be considered in career decision making.

Global Career Development

Many expatriates experience anxiety about their continued career progression. Therefore, the international experiences of expatriates must offer benefits both to the employer and to the expatriate's career as well.[9]

One global development is **repatriation,** which involves planning, training, and reassignment of global employees to their home countries. One major concern focuses on the organizational status of expatriates upon return. Many expatriates wonder what jobs they will have, whether their international experiences will be valued, and how they will be accepted back into the organization. Unfortunately, many global employers do a poor job of repatriation. To counter this problem, some companies provide career planning, the mentoring programs mentioned earlier, and even guarantees of employment upon completion of foreign assignments.

Late-Career/Retirement Issues

Whether retirement comes at age 50 or age 70, it can require a major adjustment for many people. Career development for people toward the ends of their careers may be managed in a number of ways. Phased-in retirement, consulting arrangements, and callback of some retirees as needed all act as means for gradual disengagement between the organization and the individual.

Women and Careers

The career approach for women frequently is to work hard before children arrive, step off the career track to be at home with the kids when they are young, and go back to work with a job that allows flexibility when they are older. This approach is referred to as "sequencing." But some women who sequence are concerned that the job market will not welcome them when they return, or that the time away will hurt their advancement chances. These and other career concerns provide different circumstances for many females. Employers can tap into the female labor market to a greater extent with child care, flexible work policies, and a general willingness to be accommodative.

SPECIAL CAREER ISSUES FOR ORGANIZATIONS AND INDIVIDUALS

The goals and perspectives in career planning may differ for organizations and individuals, but three issues can be problematic for both, although for different reasons. These are career plateaus (or the lack of opportunity to move up), dealing with technical professionals who do not want to go into management, and dual-career couples.

Career Plateaus

Those who do not change jobs may face another problem: career plateaus. As the baby-boomer generation reaches mid-life and beyond, and as large employers cut back on their workforces, increasing numbers of employees find themselves "stuck" at a certain career level or "plateau." This plateauing may seem like a sign of failure to some people, and plateaued employees can cause problems for employers if their frustrations affect their job performance.

Technical and Professional Workers

Technical and professional workers, such as engineers, scientists, physical therapists, and IT systems experts, present a special challenge for organizations. Many of these individuals want to stay in their technical areas rather than enter management; yet advancement in many organizations frequently requires a move into management. Most of these people like the idea of the responsibility and opportunity associated with advancement, but they do not want to leave the professional and technical puzzles and problems at which they excel.

The dual-career ladder is an attempt to solve this problem. A **dual-career ladder** is a system that allows a person to advance up either a management ladder or a corresponding ladder on the technical/professional side of a career. Dual-career ladders are now used by many firms.

Dual-Career Couples

As the number of women in the workforce, particularly in professional careers, continues to increase, so does the number of dual-career couples. Problem areas for dual-career couples include family issues and job transfers causing reloca-tions.[10] For dual-career couples with children, family issues may conflict with career progression. Thus, in job transfer situations, one partner's flexibility may depend on what is "best" for the family. Companies may consider part-time work, flextime, and work-at-home arrangements as possible options, especially for par-ents with younger children.

DEVELOPING HUMAN RESOURCES

Development represents efforts to improve employees' abilities to handle a variety of assignments and to cultivate employees' capabilities beyond those required by the current job. Development benefits both organizations and indi-viduals. Employees and managers with appropriate experiences and abilities may enhance organizational competitiveness and the ability to adapt to a changing environment. In the development process, individuals' careers also may evolve and gain new or different focuses.

Developing Specific Capabilities/Competencies

Exactly what kind of development individuals might require to expand their capabilities depends on both the individuals and the capabilities needed. One point about development is clear: in studies that asked employees what they want out of their jobs, training and development ranked at or near the top. Because the assets individuals have to sell are their knowledge, skills, and abilities, many people view the development of their KSAs as an important part of their organi-zational package. This type of development works for many but not all.

Lifelong Learning

Learning and development are closely linked. For most people, lifelong learning and development are much more likely and desirable. For many professionals, lifelong learning may mean meeting continuing education requirements to keep certified. Assistance from employers for needed lifelong development typically comes through programs at work, including tuition reimbursement programs. However, much of lifelong learning is voluntary, takes place outside work hours, and is not always formal.

Redevelopment

Whether due to a desire for career change or because the employer needs dif-ferent capabilities, people may shift jobs in mid-life or mid-career. Redeveloping or retraining people in the capabilities they need is logical and important. In the last decade, the number of college enrollees over the age of 35 has increased dra-matically. But helping employees go back to college is only one way of redeveloping them. Some companies offer redevelopment programs to recruit experienced workers from other fields. For example, different firms needing truck drivers, reporters, and IT workers have sponsored second-career programs. Public-sector employers have been using redevelopment opportunities as one recruiting tool as well.

Company Web Sites and Career Development

Many employers have Web sites, and on some of those Web sites is a section labeled "careers." The careers section can be used for many purposes, including listing open jobs for current employees looking to change jobs. The Web site is a link to the external world, but it can also be a link to existing employee development.

DEVELOPMENT NEEDS ANALYSES

Like employee training, employee development begins with analyses of the needs of both the organization and the individuals. Either the company or the individual can analyze what a given person needs to develop. The goal, of course, is to identify strengths and weaknesses. Methods that organizations use to assess development needs include assessment centers, psychological testing, and performance appraisals.

Assessment Centers

Assessment centers are collections of instruments and exercises designed to diagnose individuals' development needs. Organizational leadership uses assessment centers for both developing and selecting managers. Assessment centers provide an excellent means for determining management potential. Management and participants often praise them because they are likely to overcome many of the biases inherent in interview situations, supervisor ratings, and written tests.

Psychological Testing

Psychological pencil-and-paper tests have been used for several years to determine employees' development potential and needs. Intelligence tests, verbal and mathematical reasoning tests, and personality tests are often given. Even a test that supposedly assesses common sense is available. Psychological testing can furnish useful information on individuals about such factors as motivation, reasoning abilities, leadership style, interpersonal response traits, and job preferences.

Performance Appraisals

Well-done performance appraisals can be a source of development information. Performance data on productivity, employee relations, job knowledge, and other relevant dimensions can be gathered in such assessments. Appraisals designed for development purposes may be more useful in aiding individual employee development than appraisals designed strictly for administrative purposes.

SUCCESSION PLANNING

Planning for the succession of key executives, managers, and other employees is an important part of HR development. **Succession planning** is the process of identifying a longer-term plan for the orderly replacement of key employees. The need to replace key employees results from promotions, transfers, retirements, deaths, disabilities, departures, and other events. However, limiting succession planning just to top executive jobs is a mistake.

Succession Planning Process

Whether in small or large firms, succession planning is linked to strategic HR planning through the process shown in Figure 5.5. In this process, both the quantity and the capabilities of potential successors must be linked to organizational strategies and plans. Two coordinated activities begin the actual process of succession planning. First, the development of preliminary replacement charts ensures that the

FIGURE 5.5 Succession Planning Process

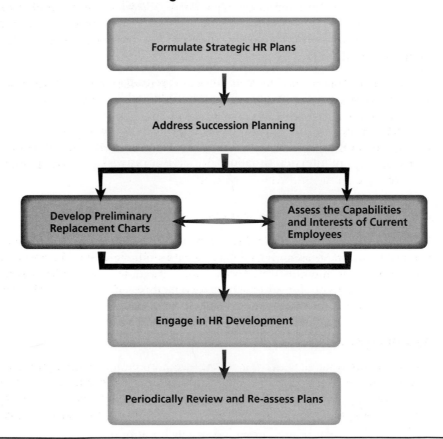

right individuals with sufficient capabilities and experience to perform the targeted jobs are available at the right time. Replacement charts (similar to depth charts used by football teams) both show the backup "players" at each position and identify positions without a current qualified backup player. The charts identify who could take over key jobs if someone leaves, retires, dies unexpectedly, or otherwise creates a vacancy. Second, assessment of the capabilities and interests of current employees provides information that can be placed into the preliminary replacement charts.

CHOOSING A DEVELOPMENT APPROACH

The most common development approaches can be categorized under two major headings: job-site development and off-site development. Both are appropriate in developing managers and other employees. Investing in human intellectual capital, whether on or off the job, becomes imperative for organizations as "knowledge work" aspects increase for almost all employers. Yet, identifying the right mix and approaches for development needs remains an art rather than a science.

Job-Site Development Approaches

All too often, unplanned and perhaps useless activities pass as development on the job. To ensure that the desired development actually occurs, managers must plan and coordinate development efforts. A number of job-site development methods can be used.

▶ **Coaching:** Training and feedback given to employees by immediate supervisors
▶ **Committee assignments:** Assigning promising employees to important committees to broaden their experiences
▶ **Job rotation:** The process of shifting a person from job to job
▶ **Online development:** Technology that provides tools for development such as using video conferencing, live chat rooms, document sharing, video and audio streaming, and Web-based courses

Off-Site Development Approaches

Off-the-job development techniques give individuals opportunities to get away from the job and concentrate solely on what is to be learned. Moreover, contact with others who are concerned with somewhat different problems and come from different organizations may provide employees with new and different perspectives. A wide variety of off-site methods are used.

Management Development

Although development is important for all employees, it is essential for managers. Effective management development imparts the knowledge and judgment needed by managers. Without appropriate development, managers may lack the capabilities to best deploy and manage resources (including employees) throughout the organization.

A number of approaches are used to mold and enhance the experience that managers need to be effective. The most widely used methods arc leadership development, management modeling, management coaching, management mentoring, supervisory development, and executive education.

NOTES

1. See *http://www.astd.org*.
2. Chan Veng Seng et al., "The Contributions of Knowledge Management to Workplace Learning," *Journal of Workplace Learning*, 14 (2002), 138–147.
3. Sharon Daniels, "Employee Training: A Strategic Approach to Better Return on Investment," *Journal of Business Strategy*, 24 (2003), 1–4.
4. Agnita D. Korsten, "Developing a Training Plan to Ensure Employees Keep Up with the Dynamics of Facility Management," *Journal of Facilities Management*, 1 (2003), 365–380.
5. Karen Evans et al., "Recognition of Tacit Skills: Sustained Learning Outcomes in Adult Learning," *International Journal of Training and Development*, 8 (2004), 54–72.
6. Svernung Skule, "Learning Conditions at Work: A Framework to Understand and Assess Informal Learning in the Work-

place," *International Journal of Training and Development*, 8 (2004), 8–20.
7. Mark E. Van Buren, *ASTD State of the Industry Report*, 2003 (Alexandria, VA: American Society of Training and Development, 2001), 11–12.
8. Andy Meisler, "Companies Weigh the Cost of Prepping Expats," *Workforce Management*, February 2004, 60–63.
9. Aldan Kelly et al., "Linking Organizational Training and Development Practices with New Forms of Career Structures," *Journal of European Industrial Training*, 27 (2003), 160.
10. Cenita Kupperbusch et al., "Predicting Husbands' and Wives' Retirement Satisfaction," *Journal of Social and Personal Relationships*, 20 (2003), 335–354; and Phyllis Moen, "Couples Work/Retirement Transitions," *Social Psychology Quarterly*, 64 (2001), 55–71.

INTERNET RESOURCES

American Society for Training and Development This Web site on training and development contains information on research, education seminars, and conferences. **http://www. astd.org**

Career Planner This Web site can assist individuals with career planning. **http://www. careerplanner. com**

SUGGESTED READINGS

Saul Carliner, *Training Design Basics*, ASTD, 2003.

John H. McConnell, *How to Identify Your Organization's Training Needs*, AMACOM, 2003.

Carolyn Nilson, *How to Manage Training*, AMACOM, 2003.

William J. Rothwell et al., *Career Planning and Succession Management*, Praeger, 2005.

Chapter 6

Performance Management and Appraisal

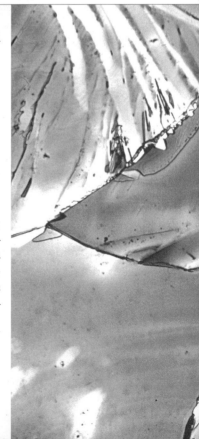

Managerial Perspectives on HR

1. Describe how an organizational culture affects a performance management system.

2. What errors might be made when preparing a performance appraisal on a clerical employee? How can these errors be avoided?

3. What should a legally defensible performance appraisal system include?

All employers want employees who perform their jobs well. However, an effective performance management system increases the likelihood that such performance will occur. A performance management system consists of the processes used to identify, encourage, measure, evaluate, improve, and reward employee performance. As shown in Figure 6.1, performance management links organizational strategy to results. The figure lists common performance management practices and outcomes in the strategy-results loop. As identified by HR professionals, a performance management system should do the following:

▶ Provide accurate information to employees about their performance.
▶ Clarify what the organization expects.
▶ Identify development needs.
▶ Document performance for personnel records.

NATURE OF PERFORMANCE MANAGEMENT

Performance management is composed of the processes used to identify, measure, communicate, develop, and reward employee performance. All performance management efforts should be driven by business strategies. Firms such as Payless ShoeSource and PPG Industries have developed performance management systems by breaking their business plans into subplans for units and departments.[1] Those plans have then served as the foundation for accomplishing the following functions:

▶ Provide information to employees about their performance.
▶ Clarify the organizational performance expectations.

▶ Identify the development steps that are needed to enhance employee performance.
▶ Document performance for personnel actions.
▶ Provide rewards for achieving performance objectives.

Difference between Performance Management and Performance Appraisals

In many organizations, managers and employees mistakenly equate performance appraisals with performance management. **Performance appraisal** is the process of evaluating how well employees perform their jobs and then communicating that information to the employees. Performance appraisal is also called *employee rating, employee evaluation, performance review,* and *performance evaluation.*

Sometimes, performance appraisal is incorrectly called *job evaluation.* Job evaluation is a compensation activity identifying the importance of jobs, whereas performance appraisal focuses on the actual performance of individuals and managers. It is easiest to think of performance appraisal as the way that performance management is implemented, as shown in Figure 6.1.

FIGURE 6.1   Performance Management System

Performance Management ⟹ Performance Appraisals ⟹ Performance Feedback ⟹ Performance Rewards and Development

---

PERFORMANCE-FOCUSED ORGANIZATIONAL CULTURE

Organizational cultures vary dramatically on many dimensions, one of which is the emphasis on performance management. Both research and organizational experiences have identified a number of components of an effective performance management system. The components are depicted in Figure 6.2. Some corporate cultures are based on *entitlement,* meaning that adequate performance and stability dominate the organization. Employee rewards systems vary little from person to person and are not based on individual performance differences. As a result, the performance appraisal activities are seen as having little tie to performance and as being primarily a "bureaucratic exercise."

At the other end of the spectrum is a *performance-driven* organizational culture focused on corporate values, results, information sharing, and performance appraisal systems that link results to employee compensation and development. The importance of a performance-focused culture is seen in the results of several studies. One longitudinal study of 207 companies in 22 industries found that firms with performance-focused cultures had significantly higher growth in company revenue, employment, net income, and stock prices than did companies with different cultures. Another study, by Becker, Huselid, and Ulrich, found that firms with strong performance cultures had dramatically better results as well.[2]

FIGURE 6.2   Components of Effective Performance Management

Executive Commitment to Performance Management

One crucial aspect of a performance-focused culture is executive involvement in continually reinforcing the performance message. If top executives do performance reviews on employees who report directly to them, then they are supporting the performance culture. In many organizations, performance appraisals are supposed to be done by all managers, but senior executives never do them, nor are they held accountable for conducting feedback with their employees.

IDENTIFYING AND MEASURING EMPLOYEE PERFORMANCE

The second phase of an effective performance management system is that important performance measures are identified and used. Employee performance measures common to most jobs include the following elements:

▶ Quantity of output
▶ Quality of output
▶ Timeliness of output
▶ Presence at work

Other dimensions of performance beyond these general ones apply to various jobs. Specific **job criteria,** or dimensions of job performance, identify the most important elements in a given job. For example, a college professor's job often includes the job criteria of teaching, research, and service. Job criteria are identified from well-written job descriptions that contain the most important factors of individual jobs. They define what the organization pays employees to do; therefore, the performance of individuals on job criteria should be measured and compared against standards, and then the results communicated to the employee.

Types of Performance Information

Managers can use three types of information about how employees are performing their jobs. *Trait-based information* identifies a character trait of the employee—such as attitude, initiative, or creativity—and may or may not be job related.

Behavior-based information focuses on specific behaviors that lead to job success. For a salesperson, the behavior "verbal persuasion" can be observed and used as information on performance.

Results-based information considers employee accomplishments. For jobs in which measurement is easy and obvious, a results-based approach works well. However, that which is measured tends to be emphasized, and that emphasis may leave out equally important but unmeasurable parts of the job.

Performance measures can also be viewed as objective or subjective. *Objective* measures can be observed directly—for example, the number of cars sold or the number of invoices processed can be counted. *Subjective* measures require judgment on the part of the evaluator and are more difficult to determine. One example of a subjective measure is a supervisor's ratings of an employee's "attitude," which cannot be seen directly. Consequently, both objective and subjective measures should be used carefully.

Relevance of Performance Criteria

Measuring performance requires the use of relevant criteria that focus on the most important aspects of employees' jobs. For example, measuring the initiative of customer service representatives in an insurance claims center may be less relevant than measuring the number of calls they handle properly. This example stresses that the most important job criteria should be identified in the employees' job descriptions.

Performance Standards

Performance standards define the expected levels of performance, and are "benchmarks" or "goals" or "targets"—depending on the approach taken. Realistic, measurable, clearly understood performance standards benefit both organizations and employees. In a sense, performance standards define what satisfactory job performance is. It is recommended that they be established *before* the work is performed. Well-defined standards ensure that everyone involved knows the levels of accomplishment expected.

Both numerical and nonnumerical standards can be established. Sales quotas and production output standards are familiar numerical performance standards.

Performance standards can be set by managers, employees, or others such as quality control inspectors or financial analysts. Generally, it is recommended that managers and supervisors review and discuss the standards with employees and get their input. The joint involvement of employees and their supervisors is critical to how the performance standards are perceived and used. Standards can be identified effectively by employees and their supervisors because both usually know what constitutes satisfactory performance of the dimensions of the employees' jobs.

LEGAL AND EFFECTIVE PERFORMANCE APPRAISAL PROCESSES

To be an effective part of performance management, performance appraisals must accomplish three major goals: legal compliance and documentation, administrative uses, and developmental uses.

Legal Concerns and Performance Appraisals

Because appraisals are supposed to measure how well employees are doing their jobs, it may seem unnecessary to emphasize that performance appraisals must be job related. Yet courts have ruled in numerous cases that performance appraisals were discriminatory and not job related. For instance, in a case involving an African American computer engineer at Hewlett-Packard, performance appraisals commended his technical skills and work efforts, but criticized his taking too much time analyzing problems. A few months after those appraisals were issued, the employee helped start a diversity group at the company. Shortly after that, his performance appraisal ratings declined, and his supervisor "encouraged" him to leave the company. The court ruled that there appeared to be enough irregularities in the performance appraisal documentation to raise questions about the fairness of the appraisal system. One concern was that the ratings were viewed as being overly subjective. A jury trial was ordered.[3]

A number of court decisions over 30 years have focused attention on performance appraisals, particularly on equal employment opportunity (EEO) concerns. The uniform guidelines issued by the Equal Employment Opportunity Commission (EEOC) and various court decisions make it clear that performance appraisals must be job related, nondiscriminatory, and documented.

Clearly, employers should have fair and nondiscriminatory performance appraisals. They should design their appraisal systems to satisfy the courts as well as performance management needs.

Uses of Performance Appraisals

Organizations generally use performance appraisals in two potentially conflicting ways. One use is to provide a measure of performance for consideration in making pay or other administrative decisions about employees. This administrative role often creates stress for managers doing the appraisals. The other use focuses on the development of individuals. In this role, the manager acts more as counselor and coach than as judge, which may change the tone of the appraisal. The developmental performance appraisal emphasizes identifying current training and development needs, as well as planning employees' future opportunities and career directions.

Administrative Uses of Appraisals Three administrative uses of appraisal impact managers and employees the most. They are: (1) determining pay adjustments (2) making job placement decisions on promotions, transfers, and demotions, and (3) choosing employee disciplinary actions up to and including termination of employment.

A performance appraisal system is often the link between additional pay and other rewards that employees receive, and their job performance. Performance-based compensation affirms the idea that pay raises are given for performance accomplishments rather than based on length of service (seniority) or granted automatically to all employees at the same percentage levels. In pay-for-performance compensation systems, historically supervisors and managers have evaluated the performance of individual employees and also made compensation recommendations for the same employees. If any part of the appraisal process fails, better-performing employees may not receive larger pay increases, and the result is perceived inequity in compensation.

Employees are interested in the other administrative uses of performance appraisal as well, such as decisions about promotions, terminations, layoffs, and transfer assignments. Promotions and demotions based on performance must be documented through performance appraisals; otherwise, legal problems can result.

Developmental Uses of Appraisals For employees, performance appraisal can be a primary source of information and feedback, which are often key to their future development. In the process of identifying employee strengths, weaknesses, potentials, and training needs through performance appraisal feedback, supervisors can inform employees about their progress, discuss areas where additional training may be beneficial, and outline future development plans. The manager's role in such a situation parallels that of a coach, discussing good performance, explaining what improvement is necessary, and showing employees how to improve. After all, many employees do not always know where and how to improve, and managers should not expect improvement if they are unwilling to provide developmental feedback.

Informal versus Systematic Appraisal Processes Performance appraisals can occur in two ways: informally and/or systematically. A superlvisor conducts an *informal appraisal* whenever necessary. The day-to-day working relationship between a manager and an employee offers an opportunity for the employee's performance to be evaluated. A manager communicates this evaluation through conversation on the job, over coffee, or by on-the-spot discussion of a specific occurrence.

Frequent informal feedback to employees can prevent "surprises" during a formal performance review. However, informal appraisal can become *too* informal. For example, a senior executive at a large firm so dreaded face-to-face evaluations that he recently delivered one manager's review while both sat in adjoining stalls in the men's room.

A *systematic appraisal* is used when the contact between manager and employee is formal, and a system is in place to report managerial impressions and observations on employee performance. One survey found that almost 90% of employers have a formal performance management system or process. Although informal appraisal is useful and necessary, it should not take the place of formal appraisal.[4]

Systematic appraisals feature a regular time interval, which distinguishes them from informal appraisals. Both employees and managers know that performance will be reviewed on a regular basis, and they can plan for performance discussions.

Timing of Appraisals Most companies require managers to conduct appraisals once or twice a year, most often annually. Employees commonly receive an appraisal 60–90 days after hiring, again at six months, and annually thereafter. "Probationary" or "introductory" employees, who are new and in a trial period, should be informally evaluated often—perhaps weekly for the first month, and monthly thereafter until the end of the introductory period. After that, annual reviews are typical.

WHO CONDUCTS APPRAISALS?

Performance appraisals can be conducted by anyone familiar with the performance of individual employees. Possible combinations include the following:

▶ Supervisors rating their employees
▶ Employees rating their superiors
▶ Team members rating each other
▶ Employees rating themselves
▶ Outside sources rating employees
▶ A variety of parties providing multisource, or 360°, feedback

The rating of employees by their immediate supervisors or managers to whom supervisors report is the most common method. The immediate superior has the main responsibility for appraisals in most organizations, although often the supervisor's boss may review and approve the appraisals. The use of teams and a concern with customer input contribute to two fast-growing sources of appraisal information: team members and parties outside the organization. Multisource (or 360°) feedback combines numerous methods and has recently grown in usage.

Supervisory Rating of Subordinates

The most widely used means of rating employees is based on the assumption that the immediate supervisor is the person most qualified to evaluate an employee's performance realistically and fairly. To help themselves provide

FIGURE 6.3   Traditional Performance Appraisal Process

accurate evaluations, some supervisors keep performance logs noting their employees' accomplishments. These logs provide specific examples to use when rating performance. Figure 6.3 shows the traditional review process by which supervisors conduct performance appraisals on employees.

Employee Rating of Managers

A number of organizations today ask employees or group members to rate the performance of supervisors and managers. A prime example of this type of rating takes place in colleges and universities, where students evaluate the performance of professors in the classroom. Performance appraisal ratings also are used for management development purposes.

Having employees rate managers provides three primary advantages. First, in critical manager/employee relationships, employee ratings can be quite useful for identifying competent managers. The rating of leaders by combat soldiers is one example of such a use. Second, this type of rating program can help make a manager more responsive to employees. This advantage can quickly become a disadvantage if the manager focuses on being "nice" rather than on managing.

A major disadvantage of having employees rate managers is the negative reaction many superiors have to being evaluated by employees. Also, the fear of reprisals may be too great for employees to give realistic ratings.

Team/Peer Rating

Having employees and team members rate each other is another type of appraisal, with potential, both to help and to hurt. Peer and team ratings are especially useful when supervisors do not have the opportunity to observe each employee's performance, but other work group members do. One challenge is how to obtain ratings from and for individuals who are on different special project teams throughout the year.

Some contend that any performance appraisal, including team/peer ratings, can negatively affect teamwork and participative management efforts. Although team members have good information on one another's performance, they may not choose to share it. They may unfairly attack, or "go easy" to spare feelings.

Self-Rating

Self-appraisal works in certain situations. As a self-development tool, it forces employees to think about their strengths and weaknesses and set goals for improvement. Employees working in isolation or possessing unique skills may be the only ones qualified to rate themselves. However, employees may not rate themselves as supervisors would rate them; they may use quite different standards.

Outsider Rating

People outside the immediate work group may be called in to conduct performance reviews. This field review approach can include someone from the HR department as a reviewer, or completely independent reviewers from outside the organization. Examples include a review team evaluating a college president, and a panel of division managers evaluating a supervisor's potential for advancement in the organization. A disadvantage of this approach is that outsiders may not know the important demands within the work group or organization.

Multisource/360° Feedback

Multisource rating, or 360° feedback, has grown in popularity. Multisource feedback recognizes that for a growing number of jobs, employee performance is multidimensional and crosses departmental, organizational, and even global boundaries. The major purpose of 360° feedback is *not* to increase uniformity by soliciting like-minded views. Instead, it is to capture evaluations of the individual employee's different roles. Figure 6.4 shows graphically some of the parties who may be involved in 360° feedback. As originally designed and used, multisource feedback focuses on the use of appraisals for future development of individuals. Conflict resolution skills, decision-making abilities, team effectiveness, communication skills, managerial styles, and technical capabilities are just some of the developmental areas that can be examined. Even in a multisource system, the

FIGURE 6.4   Multisource Appraisal

manager remains a focal point, both to receive the feedback initially and to follow up appropriately with the employee. The popularity of 360° feedback systems has led to the results being used for making compensation, promotion, termination, and other administrative decisions.

When using 360° feedback for administrative purposes, managers must anticipate potential problems. Differences among raters can present a challenge, especially in the use of 360° ratings for discipline or pay decisions. Bias can just as easily be rooted in customers, subordinates, and peers as in a boss, and the lack of accountability of those sources can affect the ratings. "Inflation" of ratings is common when the sources know that their input will affect someone's pay or career. Also, issues of the confidentiality of the input and whether it is truly kept anonymous have led to lawsuits. Even though multisource approaches to performance appraisal offer possible solutions to the well-documented dissatisfaction with performance appraisal, a number of questions arise as multisource appraisals become more common.

METHODS FOR APPRAISING PERFORMANCE

Performance can be appraised by a number of methods. Some employers use one method for all jobs and employees, some use different methods for different groups of employees, and others use a combination of methods. The following discussion highlights different methods and some of the pluses and minuses of each.

Category Scaling Methods

The simplest methods for appraising performance are category scaling methods, which require a manager to mark an employee's level of performance on a specific form divided into categories of performance. A *checklist* uses a list of statements or words from which raters check statements most representative of the characteristics and performance of employees. Often, a scale indicating perceived level of accomplishment on each statement is included, which becomes a type of graphic rating scale.

Graphic Rating Scales The **graphic rating scale** allows the rater to mark an employee's performance on a continuum. Because of its simplicity, this method is used frequently. Three aspects of performance are appraised using graphic rating scales: *descriptive categories* (such as quantity of work, attendance, and dependability), *job duties* (taken from the job description), and *behavioral dimensions* (such as decision making, employee development, and communication effectiveness).

Concerns with Graphic Rating Scales Graphic rating scales in many forms are widely used because they are easy to develop; however, they encourage errors on the part of the raters, who may depend too heavily on the form to define performance. Also, graphic rating scales tend to emphasize the rating instrument itself and its limitations. If they fit the person and the job, the scales work well. However, if they fit poorly, managers and employees who must use them frequently complain about "the rating form."

Behavioral Rating Scales In an attempt to overcome some of the concerns with graphic rating scales, employers may use behavioral rating scales, which are designed to assess an employee's *behaviors* instead of other characteristics. There are different approaches, but all describe specific examples of employee job behaviors. In a behaviorally anchored rating scale (BARS), these examples are "anchored" or measured against a scale of performance levels.

Comparative Methods

Comparative methods require that managers directly compare the performance levels of their employees against one another. For example, the Information Systems Supervisor would compare the performance of a programmer with that of other programmers. Comparative techniques include ranking and forced distribution.

Ranking The ranking method lists all employees from highest to lowest in performance. The primary drawback of the ranking method is that the sizes of the differences between individuals are not well defined. For example, the performances of individuals ranked second and third may differ little, while the performances of those ranked third and fourth differ a great deal.

Forced Distribution Forced distribution is a technique for distributing ratings that are generated with any of the other appraisal methods, and comparing the ratings of people in a work group. With the **forced distribution** method, the ratings of employees' performance are distributed along a bell-shaped curve. For example, a medical clinic administrator ranking employees on a five-point scale would have to rate 10% as a 1 ("unsatisfactory"), 20% as a 2 ("below expectations"), 40% as a 3 ("meets expectations"), 20% as a 4 ("above expectations"), and 10% as a 5 ("outstanding").

One reason why firms have mandated the use of forced distributions for appraisal ratings is to deal with "rater inflation." If employers do not require a forced distribution, performance appraisal ratings often do not approximate the normal distribution of the bell-shaped curve.

But the forced distribution method suffers from several drawbacks.[5] One problem is that a supervisor may resist placing any individual in the lowest (or the highest) group. Difficulties also arise when the rater must explain to an employee why she or he was placed in one group and others were placed in higher groups. As a result of such drawbacks, forced distribution systems have been challenged legally.

Narrative Methods

Managers and HR specialists are required to provide written appraisal information. However, some appraisal methods are entirely written. Documentation and description are the essence of the critical incident method and the essay method. In the critical incident method, the manager keeps a written record of both highly favorable and unfavorable actions performed by an employee during the entire rating period. When a "critical incident" involving an employee occurs, the manager writes it down. The critical incident method can be used with other methods to document the reasons why an employee was given a certain rating. The essay method requires a manager to write a short essay describing each employee's performance during the rating period. Some "free-form" essays are without guidelines; others are more structured, using prepared questions that must be answered.

The effectiveness of the essay approach often depends on a supervisor's writing skills. Some supervisors do not express themselves well in writing and as a result produce poor descriptions of employee performance, whereas others have excellent writing skills and can create highly positive impressions.

Management by Objectives

Management by objectives (MBO) specifies the performance goals that an individual and manager mutually identify. Each manager sets objectives derived from the overall goals and objectives of the organization; however, MBO should not be a disguised means for a superior to dictate the objectives of individual managers or employees. Other names for MBO include *appraisal by results, target coaching, work planning and review, performance objective setting,* and *mutual goal setting*.

Combinations of Methods

No single appraisal method is best for all situations. Therefore, a performance measurement system that uses a combination of methods may be sensible in certain circumstances. Using combinations may offset some of the advantages and disadvantages of individual methods. Category scaling methods sometimes are easy to develop, but they usually do little to measure strategic accomplishments. Further, they may make interrater reliability problems worse. Comparative approaches help reduce leniency and other errors, which makes them useful for administrative decisions such as determining pay raises. But comparative approaches do a poor job of linking performance to organizational goals, and they do not provide feedback for improvement as well as other methods.

Narrative methods work well for development because they potentially generate more feedback information. However, without good definitions of criteria or standards, they can be so unstructured as to be of little value. Also, these methods work poorly for administrative uses. The management-by-objectives approach works well to link performance to organizational goals, but it can require much effort and time for defining expectations and explaining the process to employees. Narrative and MBO approaches may not work as well for lower-level jobs as for jobs with more varied duties and responsibilities.

When managers can articulate what they want a performance appraisal system to accomplish, they can choose and mix methods to realize those advantages. For example, one combination might include a graphic rating scale of performance on major job criteria, a narrative of developmental needs, and an overall ranking of employees in a department. Different categories of employees (e.g., salaried exempt, salaried nonexempt, and maintenance) might require different combinations of methods.

TRAINING OF MANAGERS AND EMPLOYEES

Court decisions on the legality of performance appraisals and research on appraisal effectiveness both stress the importance of training managers and employees on performance management and conducting performance appraisals. Unfortunately, such training occurs only sporadically or not at all in many organizations.

For employees, performance appraisal training focuses on the purposes of appraisal, the appraisal process and timing, and how performance criteria and standards are linked to job duties and responsibilities. Some training also discusses how employees should rate their own performance and use that information in discussions with their supervisors and managers.

Most systems can be improved by training supervisors in doing performance appraisals.[6] Because conducting the appraisals is critical, training should center around minimizing rater errors and providing raters with details on documenting performance information.

Rater Errors

There are many possible sources of error in the performance appraisal process. One of the major sources is mistakes made by raters. Although completely eliminating these errors is impossible, making raters aware of them through training is helpful. Figure 6.5 lists some common rater errors.

FIGURE 6.5 Common Rater Errors

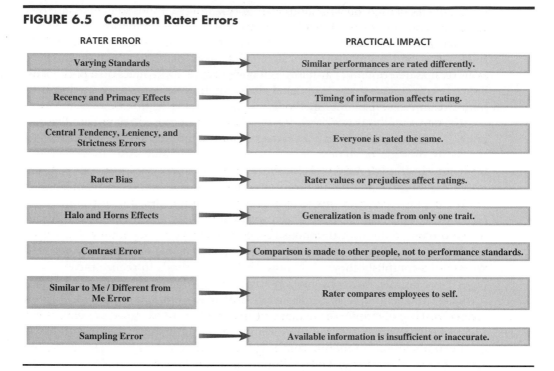

RATER ERROR	PRACTICAL IMPACT
Varying Standards	Similar performances are rated differently.
Recency and Primacy Effects	Timing of information affects rating.
Central Tendency, Leniency, and Strictness Errors	Everyone is rated the same.
Rater Bias	Rater values or prejudices affect ratings.
Halo and Horns Effects	Generalization is made from only one trait.
Contrast Error	Comparison is made to other people, not to performance standards.
Similar to Me / Different from Me Error	Rater compares employees to self.
Sampling Error	Available information is insufficient or inaccurate.

Varying Standards When appraising employees, a manager should avoid applying different standards and expectations for employees performing similar jobs. Such problems often result from the use of ambiguous criteria and subjective weightings by supervisors.

Recency and Primacy Effects The **recency effect** occurs when a rater gives greater weight to recent events when appraising an individual's performance. Giving a student a course grade based only on his performance in the last week of class, and giving a drill press operator a high rating even though she made the quota only in the last two weeks of the rating period are examples. The opposite is the **primacy effect,** which occurs when a rater gives greater weight to information received first.

Central Tendency, Leniency, and Strictness Errors Ask students, and they will tell you which professors tend to grade easier or harder. A manager may develop a similar *rating pattern.* Appraisers who rate all employees within a narrow range in the middle of the scale (i.e., rate everyone as "average") commit a **central tendency error,** giving even outstanding and poor performers an "average" rating.

   Rating patterns also may exhibit leniency or strictness. The **leniency error** occurs when ratings of all employees fall at the high end of the scale. The **strictness error** occurs when a manager uses only the lower part of the scale to rate employees. To avoid conflict, managers often rate employees higher than they should. This "ratings boost" is especially likely when no manager or HR representative reviews the completed appraisals.

Rater Bias   Rater bias occurs when a rater's values or prejudices distort the rating. Such bias may be unconscious or quite intentional. For example, a manager's dislike of certain ethnic groups may cause distortion in appraisal information for some people. Use of age, religion, seniority, sex, appearance, or other "classifications" also may skew appraisal ratings if the appraisal process is not properly designed. A review of appraisal ratings by higher-level managers may help correct this problem.

Halo and Horns Effects   The **halo effect** occurs when a rater scores an employee high on all job criteria because of performance in one area. For example, if a worker has few absences, his or her supervisor might give him or her a high rating in all other areas of work, including quantity and quality of output, without really thinking about the employee's other characteristics separately. The opposite is the *horns effect,* occurring when a low rating on one characteristic leads to an overall low rating.

Contrast Error   Rating should be done using established standards. One problem is the **contrast error,** which is the tendency to rate people relative to others rather than against performance standards. For example, if everyone else in a group performs at a mediocre level, a person performing somewhat better may be rated as "excellent" because of the contrast effect. But in a group where many employees are performing well, the same person might receive a lower rating. Although it may be appropriate to compare people at times, the performance rating usually should reflect comparison against performance standards, not against other people.

Similar to Me/Different from Me Error   Sometimes, raters are influenced by whether people show characteristics that are the same as or different from their own. For example, if a manager has an MBA degree, he might give subordinates with MBAs higher appraisals than those with only bachelor's degrees. The error comes in measuring an individual against another person rather than measuring how well the individual fulfills the expectations of the job.

Sampling Error   If the rater has seen only a small sample of the person's work, an appraisal may be subject to sampling error. For example, assume that 95% of the reports prepared by an employee have been satisfactory, but a manager sees only the 5% that has had errors. If the supervisor rates the person's performance as "poor," then a sampling error has occurred. Ideally, the work being rated should be a broad and representative sample of all the work done by the employee.

APPRAISAL FEEDBACK

After completing appraisals, managers need to communicate the results in order to give employees a clear understanding of how they stand in the eyes of their immediate superiors and the organization. Organizations commonly require managers to discuss appraisals with employees. The appraisal feedback interview provides an opportunity to clear up any misunderstandings on both sides. In this interview, the manager should focus on coaching and development, and not just tell the employee, "Here is how you rate and why." Emphasizing development gives both parties an opportunity to consider the employee's performance as part of appraisal feedback.

Appraisal Interview

The appraisal interview presents both an opportunity and a danger. It can be an emotional experience for the manager and the employee because the manager must communicate both praise and constructive criticism. A major concern for managers is how to emphasize the positive aspects of the employee's perform-ance while still discussing ways to make needed improvements. If the interview is handled poorly, the employee may feel resentment, which could lead to conflict in future working relationships.

Reactions of Managers

Managers and supervisors who must complete appraisals of their employees often resist the appraisal process. Many managers feel that their role calls on them to assist, encourage, coach, and counsel employees to improve their per-formance. However, being a judge on the one hand and a coach and a counselor on the other hand may cause internal conflict and confusion for many managers.

Knowing that appraisals may affect employees' future careers also may cause altered or biased ratings. This problem is even more likely when managers know that they will have to communicate and defend their ratings to the employees, their bosses, or HR specialists. Managers can easily avoid providing negative feedback to an employee in an appraisal interview, and thus avoid unpleasant-ness in an interpersonal situation, by making the employee's ratings positive. But avoidance helps no one. A manager owes an employee a well-done appraisal.

Reactions of Appraised Employees

Employees may well see the appraisal process as a threat and feel that the only way for them to get a higher rating is for someone else to receive a low rating. This win/lose perception is encouraged by comparative methods of rating. Emphasis on the self-improvement and developmental aspects of appraisal appears to be the most effective means to reduce these reactions from those par-ticipating in the appraisal process.

Effective Performance Management

Regardless of the approach used, managers must understand the intended out-come of performance management. When performance management is used to develop employees as resources, it usually works. When one key part of per-formance management, a performance appraisal, is used to punish employees, performance management is much less effective. In its simplest form as part of performance management, performance appraisal is a manager's observation: "Here are your strengths and weaknesses, and here is a way to develop for the future." Done well, performance management can lead to higher employee motivation and satisfaction.

NOTES

1. Kathy Goagne, "One Day at a Time: Using Performance Management to Translate Strategy into Results," *Workspan,* February 2002, 20–25.
2. Brian E. Becker, Mark A. Huselid, and Dave Ulrich, *The HR Scorecard: Linking People, Strategy, and Performance* (Boston, MA: Harvard Business School Press, 2001). Andy Meisler, "Dead Man's Curve," *Workforce Management,* July 2003, 44–49.
3. *Garrett v. Hewlett-Packard Company,* 305 F.3d 1210 (10th Cir. 2002).
4. "Performance Management Practices," *http://www.ddi.com.*
5. Michael O'Malley, "Forced Ranking," *WorldatWork Journal,* First Quarter 2003, 31–39.
6. Eileen Piggot-Irvine, "Appraisal Training Focused on What Really Matters," *International Journal of Education Management,* 17 (2003), 254.

INTERNET RESOURCES

International Society for Performance Improvement This association is dedicated to improving human performance in the workplace. The Web site includes links to many valuable articles. **http://www.ispi.org**

Performance Management Technical Assistance Center This Web site offers information on managing performance, and includes a Performance Management Handbook. **http://www. opm.gov/perform**

SUGGESTED READINGS

Robert Bacal, *Manager's Guide to Performance Reviews,* McGraw-Hill, 2003.

Robert L. Cardy, *Performance Management,* M.E. Sharpe, 2003.

Amy Delpo, *The Performance Appraisal Handbook,* NOLO, 2005.

T.V. Rao and Raju Rao, *Power of 360 Degree Feedback,* Sage Publications, 2005.

Chapter 7

Compensation Strategies and Practices

Managerial Perspectives on HR

1. What have been the consequences of the compensation philosophies and practices at organizations where you have worked?
2. If you were the HR Manager for a company with 180 employees and no formal base pay system what would you do to establish such a system?
3. Analyze the connection between executive compensation and organization performance today.

Compensation systems in organizations must be linked to organizational objectives and strategies. Employers must balance compensation costs at a level that both ensures organizational competitiveness and provides sufficient rewards to employers. In order to attract, retain, and reward employees, employers provide several types of compensation. Executive compensation practices are quite visible in many organizations; especially their linkage to organization performance.

Compensation costs represent significant expenditures in most organizations. For instance, at one large health-care organization, employee payroll and benefits expenditures constitute almost 60% of all costs. Although actual compensation costs can be easily calculated, the value derived by employers and employees proves more difficult to identify. Compensation systems in organizations must be linked to organizational objectives and strategies. Different firms have different strategies for compensation. Additionally, compensation systems must balance the interests and costs of the employers with the needs and expectations of employees.

TYPES OF COMPENSATION

Rewards can be both intrinsic and extrinsic. *Intrinsic rewards* may include praise for completing a project or meeting performance objectives. Other psychological and social forms of compensation also reflect the intrinsic type of rewards. *Extrinsic rewards* are tangible and take both monetary and nonmonetary forms. Tangible components of a compensation program are of two general types. With *direct compensation,* the employer exchanges monetary rewards for work done. Employers provide *indirect compensation*—like health insurance—to everyone simply for being members of the organization. *Base pay* and *variable pay* are the most common forms of direct compensation. Indirect compensation commonly consists of employee *benefits.*

Base Pay

The basic compensation that an employee receives, usually as a wage or a salary, is called **base pay.** Many organizations use two base pay categories, *hourly* and *salaried,* which are identified according to the way pay is distributed and the nature of the jobs. Hourly pay is the most common means and is based on time. Employees paid hourly receive **wages,** which are payments directly calculated on the amount of time worked. In contrast, people paid **salaries** receive consistent payments each period regardless of the number of hours worked.

Variable Pay

Another type of direct pay is **variable pay,** which is compensation linked directly to individual, team, or organizational performance. The most common types of variable pay for most employees are bonuses and incentive program payments. Executives often receive longer-term rewards such as stock options.

Benefits

Many organizations provide numerous extrinsic rewards in an indirect manner. With indirect compensation, employees receive the tangible value of the rewards without receiving actual cash. A **benefit** is an indirect reward—for instance, health insurance, vacation pay, or a retirement pension—given to an employee or a group of employees for organizational membership, regardless of performance, but they do not directly pay for all of that benefit.

COMPENSATION PHILOSOPHIES

Two basic compensation philosophies lie on opposite ends of a continuum, as shown in Figure 7.1. At one end of the continuum is the *entitlement* philosophy and at the other end is the *performance* philosophy. Most compensation systems fall somewhere in between.

FIGURE 7.1   Continuum of Compensation Philosophies

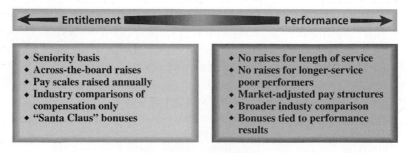

Entitlement Philosophy

The **entitlement philosophy** assumes that individuals who have worked another year are entitled to pay increases, with little regard for performance differences. Many traditional organizations that give automatic increases to their employees every year practice the entitlement philosophy. Further, most of those employees receive the same or nearly the same percentage increase each year. Commonly, in organizations with an entitlement philosophy, base pay increases are referred to as *cost-of-living* raises, even if they are not tied specifically to economic indicators.

Performance Philosophy

The **pay-for-performance philosophy** requires that compensation changes reflect individual performance differences. Organizations operating under this philosophy do not guarantee additional or increased compensation simply for completing another year of organizational service. Instead, they structure pay and incentives to reflect performance differences among employees. Employees who perform well receive larger increases in compensation; those who do not perform satisfactorily see little or no increase in compensation. Thus, employees who perform satisfactorily or better maintain or advance their positions in relation to market compensation levels, whereas poor or marginal performers may fall behind. Also, bonuses and incentives are based on individual, group, and/or organizational performance.

COMPENSATION SYSTEM DESIGN ISSUES

Depending on the compensation philosophies, strategies, and approaches identified for an organization, a number of decisions are made that affect the design of the compensation system. Some important ones are highlighted next, beginning with global issues.

Global Compensation Issues

Organizations with employees in different countries face some special compensation issues. Variations in laws, living costs, tax policies, and other factors all must be considered in establishing the compensation for local employees and managers, as well as managers and professionals brought in from other countries. Even fluctuations in the values of various monetary currencies must be tracked and adjustments made as the currencies rise or fall in relation to currency rates in other countries. With these and numerous other concerns, developing and managing a global compensation system becomes extremely complex.

Market Competitiveness and Compensation

Providing competitive compensation to employees, whether globally, domestically, or locally, is a concern for all employers. Some organizations establish specific policies about where they wish to be positioned in the labor market. These policies use

FIGURE 7.2 Compensation Quartile Strategies

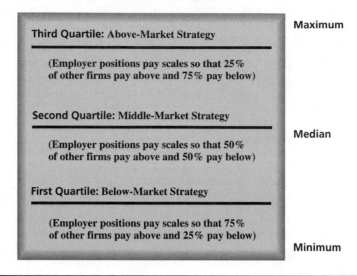

Maximum

Third Quartile: Above-Market Strategy

(Employer positions pay scales so that 25%
of other firms pay above and 75% pay below)

Second Quartile: Middle-Market Strategy

Median

(Employer positions pay scales so that 50%
of other firms pay above and 50% pay below)

First Quartile: Below-Market Strategy

(Employer positions pay scales so that 75%
of other firms pay above and 25% pay below)

Minimum

a *quartile strategy* (Figure 7.2). Data in pay surveys reveal that the dollar differential between quartiles is generally 15%–20%.

"Meet the Market" Strategy Most employers choose to position themselves in the *second quartile* (median), in the middle of the market, as identified by pay data from surveys of other employers' compensation plans. Choosing this level attempts to balance employer cost pressures and the need to attract and retain employees, by providing mid-level compensation scales that "meet the market" for the employer's jobs.

"Lag the Market" Strategy An employer using a *first-quartile* strategy may choose to "lag the market" by paying below market levels, for several reasons. If the employer is experiencing a shortage of funds, it may be unable to pay more. Also, when an abundance of workers is available, particularly those with lower skills, a below-market approach can be used to attract sufficient workers at a lesser cost. The downside of this strategy is that it increases the likelihood of higher worker turnover. If the labor market supply tightens, then attracting and retaining workers becomes more difficult.

"Lead the Market" Strategy A *third-quartile* strategy uses an aggressive approach to "lead the market." This strategy generally enables a company to attract and retain sufficient workers with the required capabilities and to be more selective when hiring. Because it is a higher-cost approach, organizations often look for ways to increase the productivity of employees receiving above-market wages.

Selecting a Quartile Deciding which quartile to position pay structures in, is a function of a number of considerations. The financial resources available, competitiveness pressures, and the market availability of employees with different capabilities are external factors. Some employers with extensive benefits programs or broad-based incentive programs may choose a first-quartile strategy, so that their overall compensation costs and levels are competitive. Other firms may have union contracts and many long-term employees that together have resulted in a third-quartile strategy. A firm in a highly competitive industry or in a remote rural location may choose to use a third-quartile strategy in order to attract and retain specialized talent. The pay levels and pay structures used can affect organizational performance.

Competency-Based Pay

The design of most compensation programs rewards employees for carrying out their tasks, duties, and responsibilities. The job requirements determine which employees have higher base rates. Employees receive more for doing jobs that require a greater variety of tasks, more knowledge and skills, greater physical effort, or more demanding working conditions. However, the design of some compensation programs emphasizes competencies rather than tasks performed.

Competency-based pay rewards individuals for the capabilities they demonstrate and acquire. Because competencies are basic capabilities that can be linked to enhanced performance, paying for competencies rewards employees who exhibit more versatility and continue to develop their competencies. In knowledge-based pay (KBP) or skill-based pay (SBP) systems, employees start at a base level of pay and receive increases as they learn to do other jobs or gain additional skills and knowledge and thus become more valuable to the employer.

Individual versus Team Rewards

As some organizations have shifted to using work teams, they face the logical concern of how to develop compensation programs that build on the team concept. The issue is how to compensate the individual whose performance may also be evaluated on the basis of team achievement. Paying everyone on a team the same amount, even though they demonstrate differing competencies and levels of performance, obviously creates concerns for many employees.

Compensation Fairness

Most people in organizations work in order to gain rewards for their efforts. Except in volunteer organizations, people expect to receive fair value, in the form of tangible compensation, for their efforts. Whether employees are considering base pay, variable pay, or benefits, the extent to which they perceive that compensation to be fair often affects their performance and how they view their jobs and employers.

Equity is the perceived fairness between what a person does (inputs) and what the person receives (outcomes). Individuals judge equity in compensation by comparing their input (effort and performance) against the effort and performance of others and against the outcomes (the rewards received). These comparisons are personal and are based on individual perceptions, not just facts. A sense of inequity occurs when the comparison suggests an imbalance between input and outcomes.

Procedural justice is the perceived fairness of the process and procedures used to make decisions about employees, including their pay. As it applies to compensation, the entire process of determining base pay for jobs, allocating pay increases, and measuring performance must be perceived as fair.

A related issue that must be considered is **distributive justice,** which is the perceived fairness in the distribution of outcomes. As one example, if a hardworking employee whose performance is outstanding receives the same across-the-board raise as an employee with attendance problems and mediocre performance, then inequity may be perceived. Likewise, if two employees have similar performance records but one receives a significantly greater pay raise, the other may perceive an inequity due to supervisory favoritism or other factors not related to the job.

Pay Secrecy versus Openness Another equity issue concerns the degree of secrecy or openness that organizations have regarding their pay systems. Pay information kept secret in "closed" systems includes how much others make, what raises others have received, and even what pay grades and ranges exist in the organization. Some firms have policies that prohibit employees from discussing their pay with other employees, and violations of these policies can lead to disciplinary action.[1] However, several court decisions have ruled that these policies violate the National Labor Relations Act. If employees who violate these "secrecy" policies are disciplined, the employers can be liable for back pay, damages, and other consequences.[2]

A number of organizations are opening up their pay systems to some degree by providing employees with more information on compensation policies, distributing a general description of the compensation system, and indicating where an individual's pay is within a pay grade. Such information allows employees to make more accurate equity comparisons. For instance, one company formerly had a pay secrecy policy, but it has discarded it and found that pay openness allows managers to manage their employees more effectively. Having a more open pay system has been found to have positive effects on employee retention and organizational effectiveness.

LEGAL CONSTRAINTS ON PAY SYSTEMS

Compensation systems must comply with many government constraints. The important areas addressed by the laws include minimum-wage standards and hours of work.

Fair Labor Standards Act (FLSA)

The major federal law affecting compensation is the Fair Labor Standards Act (FLSA), which was passed in 1938. Amended several times to raise minimum wage rates and expand the range of employers covered, the FLSA affects both private- and public-sector employers. Very small, family-owned and family-operated entities, and family farms generally remain excluded from coverage. Most federal, state, and local government employers also are subject to the provisions of the act, but military personnel, volunteer workers, and a few other limited groups are excluded.

Compliance with FLSA provisions is enforced by the Wage and Hour Division of the U.S. Department of Labor. To meet FLSA requirements, employers must keep accurate time records and maintain those records for three years. Penalties for wage and hour violations often include awards of up to two years of back pay for affected current and former employees.

Minimum Wage   The FLSA sets a minimum wage to be paid to the broad spectrum of covered employees. The actual minimum wage can be changed only by congressional action. A lower minimum wage is set for "tipped" employees, such as restaurant workers, but their compensation must equal or exceed the minimum wage when average tips are included. Minimum wage levels continue to spark significant political discussions and legislative maneuvering.

There also is a debate about the use of a living wage versus the minimum wage. A **living wage** is one that is supposed to meet the basic needs of a worker's family. In the United States, the living wage typically aligns with the amount needed for a family of four to be supported by one worker so that family income is above the officially identified "poverty" level. Currently in the United States, at about $8.20 an hour, the living-wage level is significantly higher than the minimum wage.

Exempt and Nonexempt Statuses   Under the FLSA, employees are classified as exempt or nonexempt. **Exempt employees** hold positions classified as *executive, administrative, professional,* or *outside sales,* for which employers are not required to pay overtime. **Nonexempt employees** must be paid overtime under the Fair Labor Standards Act.

In 2004, the FLSA regulations changed the terminology used to identify whether or not a job qualifies for exempt status. The categories of exempt jobs are:

▶ Executive
▶ Administrative
▶ Professional (learned or creative)
▶ Computer employees
▶ Outside sales

Overtime   The FLSA establishes overtime pay requirements. Its provisions set overtime pay at one and one-half times the regular pay rate for all hours over 40 a week, except for employees who are not covered by the FLSA. Overtime provisions do not apply to farmworkers, who also have a lower minimum-wage schedule.

The workweek is defined as a consecutive period of 168 hours (24 hours × 7 days) and does not have to be a calendar week. If they wish to do so, hospitals and nursing homes are allowed to use a 14-day period instead of a 7-day week, as long as overtime is paid for hours worked beyond 8 in a day or 80 in a 14-day period.

Compensatory Time Off   Often called *comp-time,* **compensatory time off** is hours given to an employee in lieu of payment for extra time worked. Unless it is given to nonexempt employees at the rate of one and one-half times the number of hours over 40 that are worked in a week, comp-time is illegal in the private sector. Also, comp-time cannot be carried over from one pay period to another.

FIGURE 7.3 IRS Test for Employees and Independent Contractors

An Employee	An Independent Contractor
• Must comply with instructions about when, where, and how to work • Renders services personally • Has a continuing relationship with the employer • Usually works on the premises of the employer • Normally is furnished tools, materials, and other equipment by the employer • Can be fired by the employer • Can quit at any time without incurring liability	• Can hire, supervise, and pay assistants • Generally can set own hours • Usually is paid by the job or on straight commission • Has made a significant investment in facilities or equipment • Can make a profit or suffer a loss • May provide services to two or more unrelated persons or firms at the same time • Makes services available to the public

Independent Contractor Regulations

The growing use of contingent workers by many organizations has focused attention on another group of legal regulations—those identifying the criteria that independent contractors must meet. Figure 7.3 illustrates some of the key differences between an employee and an independent contractor. The IRS considers 20 factors in making such a determination.

State and Local Laws

Many states and municipalities have enacted modified versions of federal compensation laws. If a state has a higher minimum wage than that set under the Fair Labor Standards Act, the higher figure becomes the required minimum wage in that state. On the other end of the spectrum, many states once limited the number of hours women could work. However, these laws have generally been held to be discriminatory in a variety of court cases, and states have dropped such laws.

Garnishment Laws

Garnishment occurs when a creditor obtains a court order that directs an employer to set aside a portion of an employee's wages to pay a debt owed a creditor. Regulations passed as a part of the Consumer Credit Protection Act established limitations on the amount of wages that can be garnished and restricted the right of employers to discharge employees whose pay is subject to a single garnishment order. All 50 states have laws applying to wage garnishments.

DEVELOPMENT OF A BASE PAY SYSTEM

As Figure 7.4 shows, a base compensation system is developed using current job descriptions and job specifications. These information sources are used when *valuing jobs* and analyzing *pay surveys*. These activities are designed to ensure that

FIGURE 7.4   Compensation Administration Process

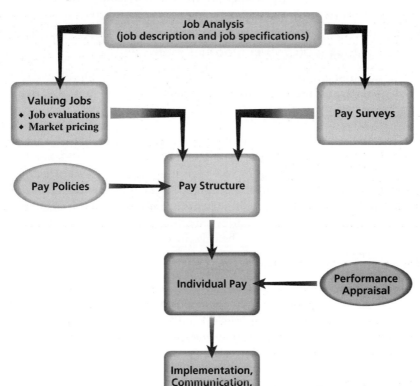

the pay system is both internally equitable and externally competitive. The data compiled in these two activities are used to design *pay structures,* including *pay grades* and minimum-to-maximum *pay ranges.* After pay structures are established, individual jobs must be placed in the appropriate pay grades and employees' pay must be adjusted according to length of service and performance. Finally, the pay system must be monitored and updated.

Employers want their employees to perceive their pay as appropriate in relation to pay for jobs performed by others inside the organization. Frequently, employees and managers make comments such as, "This job is more important than that job in another department, so why are the two jobs paid about the same?" To provide a systematic basis for determining the relative value of jobs within an organization, the employer evaluates every job in the organization on the following features:

▶ Knowledge, skills, and abilities needed to perform the job satisfactorily
▶ Nature of job tasks, duties, responsibilities, and competencies
▶ Difficulty of the job, including the physical and mental demands

Two general approaches for valuing jobs are available: job evaluation and market pricing. Both approaches are used to determine initial values of jobs in relation to other jobs in an organization.

Valuing Jobs with Job Evaluation Methods

Job evaluation is a formal, systematic means to identify the relative worth of jobs within an organization. Several job evaluation methods are available for use by employers of different sizes.

Point Method The point method is the most widely used job evaluation method. It breaks jobs down into various compensable factors and places weights, or *points,* on them. A **compensable factor** identifies a job value commonly present throughout a group of jobs. Compensable factors are derived from the job analysis. For example, for jobs in warehouse and manufacturing settings, *physical demands, hazards encountered,* and *working environment* may be identified as compensable factors and weighted heavily. In contrast, for most office and clerical jobs, these factors are of little importance and other factors are more important.

The point method has been widely used because it is relatively simple to use and it considers the components of a job rather than the total job. However, point systems have been criticized for reinforcing traditional organizational structures and job rigidity. Although not perfect, the point method of job evaluation is generally better than the classification and ranking methods because it quantifies job elements.

Valuing Jobs Using Market Pricing

A growing number of employers have scaled back their use of internal valuation through traditional job evaluation methods and switched to using market pricing more.[3] **Market pricing** uses market pay data to identify the relative value of jobs based on what other employers pay for similar jobs. Jobs are arranged in groups tied directly to similar survey data amounts. Well-known firms such as Marriott International and Dow Chemical are among employers who are relying on market pricing more and more.

Key to market pricing is identifying relevant market pay for jobs that are good "matches" with the employer's jobs, geographic considerations, and company strategies and philosophies about desired market competitiveness levels. Obviously, much of the accuracy of market pricing rests on the sources and quality of the pay surveys used.

Pay Surveys

A **pay survey** is a collection of data on compensation rates for workers performing similar jobs in other organizations. Both job evaluation and market pricing are tied to surveys of the pay that other organizations provide for similar jobs.

Because jobs may vary widely in an organization, it is particularly important to identify **benchmark jobs**—jobs that are found in many other organizations.

Often these jobs are performed by individuals who have similar duties that require similar KSAs. For example, benchmark jobs commonly used in clerical/office situations are accounts payable processor, word-processing operator, and receptionist. Benchmark jobs are used because they provide "anchors" against which individual jobs can be compared.

PAY STRUCTURES

Once job valuations and pay survey data are gathered, pay structures can be developed. Data from the valuation of jobs and the pay surveys may lead to the establishment of several different pay structures for different job families, rather than just one structure for all jobs. A **job family** is a group of jobs having common organizational characteristics. In organizations, there can be a number of different job families. Examples of some common pay structures based on different job families include (1) hourly and salaried; (2) office, plant, technical, professional, and managerial; and (3) clerical, information technology, professional, supervisory, management, and executive. The nature, culture, and structure of the organization are considerations for determining how many and which pay structures to have.

Pay Grades

In the process of establishing a pay structure, organizations use **pay grades** to group individual jobs having approximately the same job worth. Although no set rules govern establishing pay grades, some overall suggestions can be useful. Generally, 11–17 grades are used in small- and medium-sized companies, that is, companies with fewer than 500 employees.

Pay Ranges

The pay range for each pay grade also must be established. Using the market line as a starting point, the employer can determine minimum and maximum pay levels for each pay grade by making the market line the midpoint line of the new pay structure. For example, in a particular pay grade, the maximum value may be 20% above the midpoint located on the market line, and the minimum value may be 20% below it.

INDIVIDUAL PAY

Once managers have determined pay ranges, they can set the pay for specific individuals. Setting a range for each pay grade gives flexibility by allowing individuals to progress within a grade instead of having to move to a new grade each time they receive a raise. A pay range also allows managers to reward the better-performing employees while maintaining the integrity of the pay system.

Regardless of how well a pay structure is constructed, there usually are a few individuals whose pay is lower than the minimum or higher than the maximum due to past pay practices and different levels of experience and performance.

Pay Compression

One major problem many employers face is **pay compression,** which occurs when the pay differences among individuals with different levels of experience and performance become small. Pay compression occurs for a number of reasons, but the major one involves situations in which labor market pay levels increase more rapidly than current employees' pay adjustments.

In response to shortages of particular job skills in a highly competitive labor market, managers may occasionally have to pay higher amounts to hire people with those scarce skills. For example, suppose the job of specialized information systems analyst is identified as a $48,000–$68,000 salary range in one company, but qualified individuals are in short supply and other employers are paying $70,000. To fill the job the firm likely will have to pay the higher rate. Suppose also that several analysts who have been with the firm for several years started at $55,000 and have received 4% increases each year. These current employees may still be making less than the $70,000 paid to attract and retain new analysts from outside with less experience. One partial solution to pay compression is to have employees follow a step progression based on length of service, assuming performance is satisfactory or better.[4]

DETERMINING PAY INCREASES

Decisions about pay increases are often critical ones in the relationships between employees, their managers, and the organization. Individuals express expectations about their pay and about how much of an increase is "fair," especially in comparison with the increases received by other employees. There are several ways to determine pay increases, including performance, seniority, cost-of-living adjustments, and lump-sum increases. These methods can be used separately or in combination.

Pay Adjustment Matrix

Some system for integrating appraisals and pay changes must be developed and applied equally. Often, this integration is done through the development of a *pay adjustment matrix,* or *salary guide chart.* Use of pay adjustment matrices bases adjustments in part on a person's **compa-ratio,** which is the pay level divided by the midpoint of the pay range. To illustrate, the compa-ratio for two employees would be:

$$\text{Employee } R = \$16.50 \text{ (current pay)}/\$15.00 \text{ (midpoint)} \times 100$$
$$= 110 \text{ (compa-ratio)}$$

$$\text{Employee } J = \$13.05 \text{ (current pay)}/\$15.00 \text{ (midpoint)} \times 100$$
$$= 87 \text{ (compa-ratio)}$$

Salary guide charts reflect a person's upward movement in an organization. This movement often depends on the person's performance, as rated in an appraisal, and on the person's position in the pay range, which has some relation to experience as well. A person's placement on the chart determines what

FIGURE 7.5 Pay Adjustment Matrix

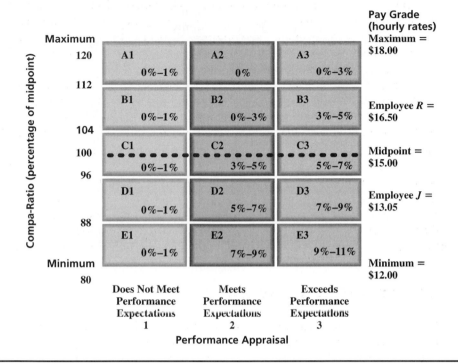

pay raise the person should receive. For example, if employee *J* is rated as exceeding expectations[2] with a compa-ratio of 87, that person is eligible for a raise of 7%–9%, according to the chart in Figure 7.5. Two interesting facets of the sample matrix illustrate the emphasis on paying for performance. First, individuals whose performance is below expectations receive small to no raises, not even a so-called cost-of-living raise. This approach sends a strong signal that poor performers will not continue to receive increases just by completing another year of service.

Second, as employees move up the pay range, they must exhibit higher performance to obtain the same percentage raise as those lower in the range performing at the "meets performance expectations" level. This approach is taken because the firm is paying above the market midpoint but receiving only satisfactory performance rather than above-market performance. Charts can be constructed to reflect the specific pay-for-performance policy and philosophy in an organization.

Seniority/COLAS/LSI

Seniority, or time spent in the organization or on a particular job, can be used as the basis for pay increases. Many employers have policies that require a person to be employed for a certain length of time before being eligible for pay increases. Pay adjustments based on seniority often are set as automatic steps once a person has been employed the required length of time, although performance must be at least satisfactory in many nonunion systems.

A common pay-raise practice is the use of a *cost-of-living adjustment (COLA)*. Often, these adjustments are tied to changes in the Consumer Price Index (CPI) or some other general economic measure. However, numerous studies have revealed that the CPI overstates the actual cost of living.

Most employees who receive pay increases, either for merit or for seniority, first receive an increase in the amount of their regular monthly or weekly paycheck. For example, an employee who makes $12.00 an hour and then receives a 3% increase will move to $12.36 an hour.

In contrast, a **lump-sum increase (LSI)** is a one-time payment of all or part of a yearly pay increase. The pure LSI approach does not increase the base pay. Therefore, in the example of a person making $12.00 an hour, if an LSI of 3% is granted, then the person receives a lump sum of $748.80 ($0.36 an hour × 2,080 working hours in the year). However, the base rate remains at $12.00 an hour, which slows down the progression of the base wages. The firm can vary the amount of the "lump" from one year to the next, without having to continually raise the base rate.

EXECUTIVE COMPENSATION

Many organizations, especially large ones, administer compensation for executives differently from compensation for lower-level employees. At the heart of most executive compensation plans is the idea that executives should be rewarded if the organization grows in profitability and value over a period of years. Therefore, variable pay distributed through different types of incentives is a significant part of executive compensation.

Global Executive Compensation

Executive compensation packages vary significantly from country to country. In multinational firms, the differences may be less pronounced because executives are often part of global corporate compensation plans. In comparable-size firms in Europe and the United States, total cash compensation for Chief Executive Officers (CEOs) is similar, about $2.5 million a year. But long-term incentives are used more in French and German companies than in the United Kingdom. Scandinavian firms pay their CEOs about 30% less than do other European firms.[5] Also, Japanese CEOs are paid about one-third of what U.S. CEOs in comparable-size firms are paid.[6] Critics of executive pay levels point out that in the United States, many corporate CEOs make almost 200 times more than do average workers in their firms, up from 35 times more in the 1970s. In Japan, the ratio is 15:1, and in Europe, 20:1.

Elements of Executive Compensation

Because high-salaried executives are in higher tax brackets, many executive compensation packages are designed to offer significant tax savings. These savings occur through use of deferred compensation methods whereby taxes are not due until after the executives leave the firm. According to a review of the compensation packages of CEOs of 350 large companies, long-term incentives constitute 68% of the total CEO compensation.[7]

Executive Salaries Salaries of executives vary by the type of job, size of organization, industry, and other factors. In some organizations, particularly non-profits, salaries often make up 90% or more of total compensation. In contrast, in large corporations, salaries may constitute 30% or less of the total package. Survey data on executive salaries are often reviewed by Boards of Directors to ensure that their organizations are competitive.

Executive Benefits Many executives are covered by *regular benefits plans* that are also available to nonexecutive employees, including traditional retirement, health insurance, and vacations plans. In addition, executives may receive *supplemental benefits* that other employees do not receive. For example, executive health plans with no co-payments and with no limitations on deductibles or physician choice are popular among small- and middle-size businesses. Corporate-owned insurance on the life of the executive is also popular; this insurance pays both the executive's estate and the company in the event of death. One supplemental benefit that has grown in popularity is company-paid financial planning for executives. Trusts of various kinds may be designed by the company to help the executives deal with estate-planning and tax issues. Deferred compensation is another possible means of helping executives with tax liabilities caused by incentive compensation plans.

Executive Perquisites (Perks) In addition to the regular benefits received by all employees, executives often receive benefits called perquisites. **Perquisites (perks)** are special benefits—usually noncash items—for executives. Many executives value the status enhancement of these visible symbols, which allow them to be seen as "very important people" both inside and outside their organizations. Perks can also offer substantial tax savings because some of them are not taxed as income. Some commonly used executive perks are company cars, health club and country club memberships, first-class air travel, use of private jets, stress counseling, and chauffer services.

Annual Executive Incentives and Bonuses Annual incentives and bonuses for executives can be determined in several ways. One way is to use a discretionary system whereby the CEO and the Board of Directors decide bonuses; the absence of formal, measurable targets detracts significantly from this approach. Another way is to tie bonuses to specific measures, such as return on investment, earnings per share, and net profits before taxes. More complex systems create bonus pools and thresholds above which bonuses are computed. Whatever method is used, it is important to describe it so that executives attempting to earn additional compensation understand the plan; otherwise, the incentive effect will be diminished.

Performance Incentives: Long-Term versus Short-Term   Use of executive performance-based incentives try to tie executive compensation to long-term growth and success of the organization. However, whether these incentives really emphasize the long-term or merely represent a series of short-term rewards is controversial. Short-term rewards based on quarterly or annual performance may not result in the kind of long-run-oriented decisions necessary for the company to perform well over multiple years.

As would be expected, the total amount of pay-for-performance incentives varies by management level, with CEOs receiving significantly more than subsidiary or other senior managers. The typical CEO gets about half of all the total incentives paid to all senior managers and executives.

The most widely used long-term incentives are stock option plans. A stock option gives individuals the right to buy stock in a company, usually at an advantageous price. Despite the prevalence of such plans, research has found little relationship between providing CEOs with stock options and subsequent firm performance. Because of the numerous corporate scandals involving executives at Enron, WorldCom, Tyco, and others who received outrageously high compensation due to stock options, the use of stock options has declined. Instead, more firms with publicly traded stock are using means such as *restricted stock, phantom stock, performance shares,* and other specialized technical forms, which are beyond the scope of this discussion.

Another outcome of the recent corporate abuses by executives was the passage of the Sarbanes-Oxley Act of 2002. This act has numerous provisions that have affected the accounting and financial reporting requirements of different types of executive compensation. Also, the Financial Accounting Standards Board (FASB) has adopted rules regarding the expensing of stock options. Microsoft and IBM have been leaders in restructuring stock plans.

Reasonableness of Executive Compensation

The notion that monetary incentives tied to performance result in improved performance makes sense to most people. However, there is an ongoing debate about whether executive compensation in the United States is truly linked to performance. This is particularly of concern given the astronomical amounts of some executive compensation packages, as highlighted in the HR Perspective.

The reasonableness of executive compensation is often justified by comparison to compensation market surveys, but these surveys usually provide a range of compensation data that requires interpretation. Various questions have been suggested for determining if executive pay is reasonable, including the following useful ones:

► Would another company hire this person as an executive?
► How does the executive's compensation compare with that for executives in similar companies in the industry?

► Is the executive's pay consistent with pay for other employees within the company?

► What would an investor pay for the level of performance of the executive?

Linkage between Executive Compensation and Corporate Performance Of all the executive compensation issues that are debated, the one discussed most frequently is whether or not executive compensation levels are sufficiently linked to organizational performance. In many settings, financial measures such as return on equity, return to shareholders, earnings per share, and net income before taxes are used to measure performance. However, a number of firms also incorporate nonfinancial organizational measures of performance when determining executive bonuses and incentives. Customer satisfaction, employee satisfaction, market share, productivity, and quality are other areas measured for executive performance rewards.

One of the more controversial issues is that some executives seem to get large awards for negative actions. It seems contradictory from an employee's perspective to reward executives who often improve corporate results by cutting staff, laying off employees, changing pension plans, or increasing the deductible on the health insurance. But sometimes cost-cutting measures are necessary to keep a company afloat. However, a sense of reasonableness may be appropriate too; if rank and file employees suffer, giving bonuses and large payouts to executives appears counterproductive, and even hypocritical.

Executive Compensation and Boards of Directors In most organizations, the Board of Directors is the major policy-setting entity and must approve executive compensation packages. The **compensation committee** usually is a subgroup of the Board, composed of directors who are not officers of the firm. Compensation committees generally make recommendations to the Board of Directors on overall pay policies, salaries for top officers, supplemental compensation such as stock options and bonuses, and additional perquisites for executives.

NOTES

1. Jonathan A. Segal, "Labor Pains for Union-Free Employers," *HR Magazine,* March 2004, 113–118.

2. Rafael Gely and Leonard Bierman, "Pay Secrecy/Confidentiality Rules and the National Labor Relations Act," *Journal of Labor and Employment Law,*

3. Brian Hinchcliffe, "The Juggling Act: Internal Equity and Market Pricing," *Workspan,* February 2003, 46–48.

4. Andrew L. Klein, Kimberly M. Keating, and Lisa M. Ruggerio, "The Perils of Pay Inequity: Addressing the Problems of Compression," *WorldatWork Journal,* Fourth Quarter 2002, 56–62.

5. "Pay Packages of European Execs Reach U.S. Levels," January 21, 2004, *http://www. haygroup.com.*

6. Louis Aguilar, "Exec-Worker Pay Gap Widens to Gulf," *The Denver Post,* July 8, 2001, 16A.

7. "The WSJ/Mercer 2003 CEO Compensation Survey," *Wall Street Journal,* April 12, 2004, R6; and *The Mercer Report,* May 2004.

INTERNET RESOURCES

Wage and Hour Division This government Web site from the Wage and Hour Division of the U.S. Department of Labor provides an overview of the exemptions under the Fair Labor Standards Act. **http://www.dol.gov/esa/regs**

World at Work Formerly the American Compensation Association, this Web site lists products, services, and research on compensation and benefits. **http://www.worldatwork.org**

SUGGESTED READINGS

Michael Davis, *Executive Compensation,* WorldatWork, 2004.

Robert L. Heneman, Strategic *Reward Management*, Information Age Publishing, 2002.

Brent M. Longnecker, *Rethinking Strategic Compensation*, CCH, 2004.

Todd Manas and Michael Dennis Graham, *Creating a Total Rewards Strategy*, AMACOM, 2003.

Chapter 8

Variable Pay and Benefits

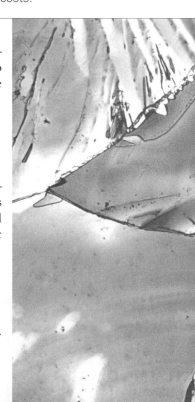

Employers increasingly are recognizing that the definition of total compensation must be extended beyond base pay to include variable pay and employee benefits. While adding value to employees, variable pay and benefits can add significant costs to employers. The increase in health insurance costs is a glaring example for most employers.

Pay-for-performance is being utilized by a growing number of employers. In today's competitive global economy, many employers believe that people become more productive if compensation varies directly according to performance. A significant number of employers are adding to their traditional base pay programs by offering employees additional compensation. The amount of payment varies based on the degree to which individual, group/team, and organizational performance goals are attained.

VARIABLE PAY: INCENTIVES FOR PERFORMANCE

Variable pay is compensation linked to individual, group/team, and/or organizational performance. Traditionally also known as *incentives,* variable pay plans attempt to provide tangible rewards to employees for performance beyond normal expectations. The philosophical foundation of variable pay rests on several basic assumptions:

▶ Some jobs contribute more to organizati onal success than others.
▶ Some people perform better and are more productive than others.
▶ Employees who perform better should receive more compensation.
▶ Some of employees' total compensation should be tied directly to performance.

In the case of pay-for-performance plans, one size does not fit all. A plan that has worked well for one company will not necessarily work well for another. Obviously, the plan must be linked to the objectives of the organization.[1]

Measuring the Success of Variable Pay Plans

The results of variable pay plans, like those in other areas of HR, should be measured to determine the success of the programs. Different measures of success can be used, depending on the nature of the plan and the goals set for it. Figure 8.1 shows some examples of different measures that may be used to evaluate variable pay plans.

Successes and Failures of Variable Pay Plans

Even though variable pay has grown in popularity, some attempts to implement it have succeeded and others have not. Incentives *do* work, but they are not a panacea because their success depends on the circumstances.

The positive view that many employers have for variable pay is not shared universally by all employees. If individuals see incentives as desirable, they are more likely to put forth the extra effort to attain the performance objectives that trigger the incentive payouts. As one indicator, a survey of employees found that only 29% believe that they are rewarded when doing a good job. Discouragingly for firms with incentive plans, approximately the same low percentage of employees indicated that they were motivated by their employers' incentive plans.[2] One problem is that many employees prefer that performance rewards increase their base pay, rather than be given as a one-time, lump-sum payment. Further, many employees prefer individual rewards to group/team or organizational incentives.

FIGURE 8.1 Metrics for Variable Pay Plans

Strategic and Financial Programs	Sales Programs	HR Programs
◆ Revenue growth before/after plan ◆ Return on investment (plan results ÷ plan costs) ◆ Profit margin improvement	◆ Increase in market share ◆ Acquisition of new customers ◆ Growth in existing customer sales ◆ Customer satisfaction levels	◆ Employee satisfaction surveys ◆ Turnover cost reduction ◆ Reduced absenteeism ◆ Decline in worker's compensation claims ◆ Decrease in accidents/injuries

INDIVIDUAL INCENTIVES

Individual incentive systems try to tie individual effort to additional rewards. Conditions necessary for the use of individual incentive plans are as follows:

▶ *Individual performance must be identified:* The performance of each individual must be measured and identified because each employee has job responsibilities and tasks that can be separated from those of other employees.
▶ *Independent work must be performed:* Individual contributions result from independent work and effort given by individual employers.
▶ *Individual competitiveness must be desired:* Because individuals generally pursue the incentives for themselves, competition among employees often occurs. Therefore, independent competition in which some individuals "win" and others do not must be desired.
▶ *Individualism must be stressed in the organizational culture:* The culture of the organization must be one that emphasizes individual growth, achievements, and rewards. If an organization emphasizes teamwork and cooperation, then individual incentives may be counterproductive.

Piece-Rate Systems

The most basic individual incentive systems are piece-rate systems, whether straight or differential. Under the **straight piece-rate system,** wages are determined by multiplying the number of units produced (such as garments sewn or service calls handled) by the piece rate for one unit. Because the cost is the same for each unit, the wage for each employee is easy to figure, and labor costs can be accurately predicted. A *differential piece-rate system* pays employees one piece-rate wage for units produced up to a standard output and a higher piece-rate wage for units produced over the standard. Many possible combinations of straight and differential piece-rate systems can be used, depending on situational factors.

Despite their incentive value, piece-rate systems are difficult to apply because determining standards is a complex and costly process for many types of jobs. In some instances, the cost of determining and maintaining the standards may be greater than the benefits derived. Also, jobs in which individuals have limited control over output or in which high standards of quality are necessary may be unsuited to piecework.

Bonuses

Individual employees may receive additional compensation in the form of a **bonus,** which is a one-time payment that does not become part of the employee's base pay. Growing in popularity, individual bonuses are used at all levels in some firms.

A bonus can recognize performance by an employee, a team, or the organization as a whole. When performance results are good, bonuses go up. When performance results are not met, bonuses go down. Most employers base part of an employee's bonus on individual performance and part on company results, as appropriate.

Special Incentive Programs

Numerous special incentive programs have been used to reward individuals, ranging from one-time contests for meeting performance targets to awards for performance over time. For instance, safe-driving awards are given to truck drivers with no accidents or violations on their records during a year. Although special programs can be developed for groups and for entire organizations, they often focus on rewarding only high-performing individuals.

SALES COMPENSATION

The compensation paid to employees involved with sales and marketing is partly or entirely tied to individual sales performance. Salespeople who sell more receive more total compensation than those who sell less. Sales incentives are perhaps the most widely used individual incentives.

Types of Sales Compensation Plans

Sales compensation plans can be of several general types, depending on the degree to which total compensation includes some variable pay tied to sales performance. A look at three general types of sales compensation and some challenges to sales compensation follows.

Salary-Only Some companies pay salespeople only a salary. The *salary-only approach* is useful when an organization emphasizes serving and retaining existing accounts, over generating new sales and accounts. This approach is frequently used to protect the income of new sales representatives for a period of time while they are building up their sales clientele. Generally, the employer extends the salary-only approach for new sales representatives to no more than six months, at which point it implements a salary-plus-commission or salary-plus-bonuses system.

Straight Commission An individual incentive system that is widely used in sales jobs is the **commission,** which is compensation computed as a percentage of sales in units or dollars. Commissions are integrated into the pay given to sales workers in three common ways: straight commission, salary-plus-commission, and bonuses.

In the *straight commission system,* a sales representative receives a percentage of the value of the sales made. The advantage of this system is that it requires sales representatives to sell in order to earn. The disadvantage is that it offers no security for the sales staff.

Salary-Plus-Commission or Bonuses The form of sales compensation used most frequently is the *salary-plus-commission,* which combines the stability of a salary with the performance aspect of a commission. A common split is 70% salary to 30% commission, although the split varies by industry and by numerous other factors. Many organizations also pay salespeople salaries and then offer bonuses that are a percentage of the base pay, tied to how well the employee meets various sales targets or other criteria.

Sales Compensation Challenges

Sales incentives work well, especially when they are tied to strategic initiatives of the organization. However, they do present many challenges—from calculating total pay correctly, to dealing with sales in e-business, to causing competition among salespeople. Often, sales compensation plans become quite complex, and tracking individual incentives can be demanding. Internet-based software has helped because companies can use it to post results daily, weekly, or monthly and salespeople can use it to track their results.

Sales Performance Metrics Successfully using variable sales compensation requires establishing clear performance criteria and measures. Generally, no more than three sales performance measures should be used in a sales compensation plan. Consultants criticize many sales commission plans as being too complex to motivate sales representatives. Other plans may be too simple, focusing only on the salesperson's pay, not on organizational objectives. Many companies measure performance primarily by comparing an individual's sales revenue against established quotas. The plans would be better if the organizations used a variety of criteria, including obtaining new accounts and selling high-value versus low-value items that reflect marketing plans.

GROUP/TEAM INCENTIVES

The use of groups/teams in organizations has implications for compensation. Although the use of groups/teams has increased substantially in the past few years, the question of how to compensate their members equitably remains a significant challenge. According to several studies, about 80% of large firms provide rewards for work groups or teams in some way.[3]

Design of Group/Team Incentive Plans

In designing group/team incentive plans, organizations must consider a number of issues. The main concerns are how and when to distribute the incentives, and who will make decisions about the incentive amounts.

Distribution of Group/Team Incentives Several decisions about how to distribute and allocate group/team rewards must be made. The two primary ways for distributing those rewards are as follows:

1. *Same-size reward for each member:* With this approach, all members receive the same payout, regardless of job level, current pay, seniority, or individual performance differences.
2. *Different-size reward for each member:* With this approach, employers vary individual rewards depending on such factors as contribution to group/team results, current pay, years of experience, and skill levels of jobs performed.

Generally, more organizations use the first approach in addition to different levels of individual pay. The combination rewards performance by making the group/team incentive equal, while still recognizing that individual pay differences exist and are important to many employees. The size of the group/team incentive can be determined either by using a percentage of base pay for the individuals or the group/team as a whole, or by offering a specific dollar amount.

Problems with Group/Team Incentives

The difference between rewarding team members *equally* and rewarding them *equitably* triggers many of the problems associated with group/team incentives. Generally, managers view the concept of people working in groups/teams as beneficial. But many employees still expect to be paid according to individual performance, to a large extent. Until this individualism is recognized and compensation programs that are viewed as more equitable by more "team members" are developed, caution should be used in creating and implementing group/team incentives.

Successes and Failures of Group/Team Incentives

The unique nature of each group/team and its members figures prominently in the success of establishing incentive rewards. The employer must consider the history of the group and its past performance. Another consideration for the success of these incentives is the number of employees in the group/team. If it becomes too large, employees may feel that their individual efforts will have little or no effect on the total performance of the group and the resulting rewards. But group/team incentive plans may encourage cooperation in small groups where interdependence is high. Therefore, in those groups, the use of group/team performance measures is recommended. Such plans have been used in many industries. Conditions for successful team incentives are shown in Figure 8.2. If these conditions cannot be met, then either individual or organizational incentives may be more appropriate.

Types of Group/Team Incentives

Group/team reward systems use various ways of compensating individuals. The components include individual wages and salaries in addition to the additional rewards. Most organizations using group/team incentives continue to pay indi-

FIGURE 8.2   Conditions for Successful Group/Team Incentives

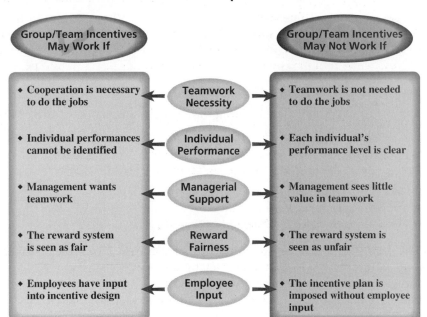

viduals based either on the jobs performed or the individuals' competencies and capabilities. The two most frequently used types of group/team incentives situations are work team results and gainsharing.

Group/Team Results Pay plans for groups/teams may reward all members equally on the basis of group output, cost savings, or quality improvement. The design of most group/team incentives is based on a "self-funding" principle, which means that the money to be used as incentive rewards is obtained through improvement of organizational results. A good example is gainsharing, which can be extended within a group or plantwide.

Gainsharing The system of sharing with employees greater-than-expected gains in profits and/or productivity is **gainsharing.** To develop and implement a gainsharing or goalsharing plan, management must identify the ways in which increased productivity, quality, and financial performance can occur and decide that some of the gains should be shared with employees. Often, measures such as labor costs, overtime hours, and quality benchmarks are used. Both organizational measures and departmental measures may be used, with the weights for gainsharing split between the two categories. Plans frequently require that an individual must exhibit satisfactory performance to receive the gainsharing payments.

ORGANIZATIONAL INCENTIVES

An organizational incentive system compensates all employees in the organization according to how well the organization as a whole performs during the year.

Profit Sharing

As the name implies, **profit sharing** distributes some portion of organizational profits to employees. The primary objectives of profit-sharing plans include the following:

▶ Increase productivity and organizational performance.
▶ Attract or retain employees.
▶ Improve product/service quality.
▶ Enhance employee morale.

Typically, the percentage of the profits distributed to employees is set by the end of the year before distribution. In some profit-sharing plans, employees receive portions of the profits at the end of the year; in others, the profits are deferred, placed in a fund, and made available to employees on retirement or on their departure from the organization.

When used throughout an organization, including with lower-echelon workers, profit-sharing plans can have some drawbacks. Employees must trust that management will disclose accurate financial and profit information. As many people know, both the definition and level of profit can depend on the accounting system used and on decisions made. To be credible, management must be willing to disclose sufficient financial and profit information to alleviate the skepticism of employees, particularly if profit-sharing levels fall from those of previous years.

Employee Stock Plans

Two types of organizational incentive plans use employer stock ownership to reward employees. The goal of these plans is to get employees to think and act like "owners."

A **stock option plan** gives employees the right to purchase a fixed number of shares of company stock at a specified exercise price for a limited period of time. If the market price of the stock exceeds the exercise price, employees can then exercise the option and buy the stock. The number of firms giving stock options to nonexecutives has declined some in recent years, primarily due to changing laws and accounting regulations.

An **employee stock ownership plan (ESOP)** is designed to give employees significant stock ownership in their employers. Establishing an ESOP creates several advantages. The major one is that the firm can receive favorable tax treatment on the earnings earmarked for use in the ESOP. Another is that an ESOP gives employees a "piece of the action" so that they can share in the growth and profitability of their firm. Employee ownership may motivate employees to be more productive and focused on organizational performance.

STRATEGIC PERSPECTIVES ON BENEFITS

Employers provide benefits to their workers for being part of the organization. A **benefit** is an indirect reward given to an employee or a group of employees for organizational membership. Benefits often include retirement plans, vacations with pay, health insurance, educational assistance, and many more programs.

Benefits are costly for the typical U.S. employer. They average over 40% of payroll expenses for employers, and in highly unionized manufacturing and utility industries, they may be as high as 80% of payroll.

Benefits as Competitive Advantage

Employers offer some benefits to aid recruiting and retention, some because they are required to do so, and some simply because doing so reinforces the company philosophy of social and corporate citizenship. Employers with good benefits are viewed positively within a community and the industry by customers, civic leaders, current employees, and workers in other firms. Conversely, the employers who are seen as skimping on benefits, cutting benefits, or taking advantage of workers may be viewed negatively.

Benefits and Workforce Attraction/Retention

The composition of the U.S. workforce is changing, and expectations about benefits of different generations of employees are affecting benefit decisions. For instance, in some organizations many "baby boomers" who are approaching retirement age are more concerned about retirement benefits and health care. The younger-generation workers are more interested in portable flexible benefits. However, all generations expect medical and dental insurance. Having benefits plans that appeal to the different groups is vital to attracting and retaining all employees.

Benefits Design

Benefits plans can provide flexibility and choices for employees, or can be standardized for all employees. Increasingly, employers are finding that providing employees with some choices and flexibility allows individuals to tailor their benefits to their own situations. However, the more choices available, the more administrative demands placed on organizations.

TYPES OF BENEFITS

A wide range of benefits are offered by employers. Some are mandated by laws and government regulations, while others are offered voluntarily by employers as part of their HR strategies.

Government-Mandated Benefits

There are many mandated benefits that employers in the United States must provide to employees by law. Social Security and unemployment insurance are funded through a tax paid by the employer based on the employee's compensation. Workers' compensation laws exist in all states. In addition, under the Family and Medical Leave Act (FMLA), employers must offer unpaid leave to employees with certain medical or family difficulties. Other mandated benefits are funded in part by tax, through Social Security. The Consolidated Omnibus Budget Reconciliation Act (COBRA) mandates that an employer must continue health-care coverage paid for by the employees after they leave the organization. The Health Insurance Portability and Accountability Act (HIPAA) requires that most employees be able to obtain coverage if they were previously covered in a health plan and provides privacy rights for medical records.

Voluntary Benefits

Employers voluntarily offer other types of benefits to compete for and retain employees. By offering additional benefits, organizations are recognizing the need to provide greater security and benefits support to workers with widely varied personal circumstances. In addition, as jobs become more flexible and varied, both workers and employers recognize that choices among benefits are necessary, as evidenced by the growth in flexible benefits and cafeteria benefit plans. Figure 8.3 lists seven types of mandated and voluntary benefits. The following sections describe them by type.

SECURITY BENEFITS

A number of benefits provide employee security. These benefits include some mandated by laws and others offered by employers voluntarily. The primary benefits found in most organizations include workers' compensation, unemployment compensation, and severance pay.

Workers' Compensation

Workers' compensation provides benefits to persons injured on the job. State laws require most employers to supply workers' compensation coverage by purchasing insurance from a private carrier or state insurance fund or by providing self-insurance. U.S. government employees are covered under the Federal Employees Compensation Act, administered by the U.S. Department of Labor.

The workers' compensation system requires employers to give cash benefits, medical care, and rehabilitation services to employees for injuries or illnesses occurring within the scope of their employment. In exchange, employees give up the right of legal actions and awards. The costs to employers for workers' compensation average about 2.2% of total payroll, and cost about $1.68 per $100 in wages per worker.[4]

FIGURE 8.3   Types of Benefits

Security	Health Care	Family Oriented
◆ Workers' compensation ◆ Unemployment compensation	◆ COBRA and HIPAA provisions	◆ FMLA provisions
◆ Supplemental unemployment benefits (SUBs) ◆ Severance pay	◆ Medical and dental ◆ Prescription drugs ◆ Vision ◆ PPO, HMO, and CDH plans ◆ Wellness programs ◆ Flexible spending accounts	◆ Adoption benefits and dependent-care assistance ◆ Domestic partner benefits
Retirement		**Time Off**
◆ Social Security ◆ ADEA and OWBPA provisions		◆ Military reserve time off ◆ Election and jury leaves
Financial		
◆ Early retirement options ◆ Health care for retirees ◆ Pension plans ◆ Individual retirement accounts (IRAs) ◆ Keogh plans ◆ 401 (k), 403 (b), and 457 plans	◆ Financial services (e.g., credit unions and counseling) ◆ Relocation assistance ◆ Life insurance ◆ Disability insurance ◆ Long-term care insurance ◆ Legal insurance ◆ Educational assistance	◆ Lunch and rest breaks ◆ Holidays and vacations ◆ Family leave ◆ Medical and sick leave ◆ Paid time off ◆ Funeral and bereavement leaves
		Miscellaneous
		◆ Social and recreational programs and events ◆ Unique programs

Unemployment Compensation

Another benefit required by law is unemployment compensation, established as part of the Social Security Act of 1935. Because each U.S. state operates its own unemployment compensation system, provisions differ significantly from state to state.

Severance Pay

Severance pay is a security benefit voluntarily offered by employers to the employees who lose their jobs. Severed employees may receive lump-sum severance payments if their employment is terminated by the employer. For example, if a facility closes because it is outmoded and no longer economically profitable to operate, the employees who lose their jobs may receive lump-sum payments based on their years of service. Severance pay provisions often provide higher severance payments corresponding to an employee's level within the organization and the person's years of employment.

RETIREMENT BENEFITS

The aging of the workforce in many countries is affecting retirement planning for individuals and retirement plan costs for employers and governments. In the United States, the number of citizens at least 55 years or older will increase 46% between 2004 and 2010, and older citizens will constitute 38% of the population in

2010. Simultaneously, the age of retirement will decline, as it has been for decades. With more people retiring earlier and living longer, retirement benefits are becoming a greater concern for employers, employees, and retired employees.

Retirement Benefits and Age Discrimination

According to a 1986 amendment to the Age Discrimination in Employment Act (ADEA), most employees cannot be forced to retire at a specific age. As a result, employers have had to develop policies to comply with these regulations. In many employer pension plans, "normal retirement" is the age at which employees can retire and collect full pension benefits. Employers must decide whether individuals who continue to work past normal retirement age (perhaps 65) should receive the full benefits package, especially pension credits.

Retiree Benefits Some employers choose to offer their retirees benefits, which may be paid for by the retirees, the company, or both. These benefits are usually available until the retiree is eligible for Medicare. The costs of such coverage have risen dramatically. To ensure that firms adequately reflect the liabilities for retiree health benefits, the Financial Accounting Standards Board (FASB) issued Rule 106, which requires employers to establish accounting reserves for funding retiree health-care benefits.

Social Security

The Social Security Act of 1935, with its later amendments, established a system providing *old-age, survivor's, disability,* and *retirement* benefits. Administered by the federal government through the Social Security Administration, this program provides benefits to previously employed individuals. Employees and employers share in the cost of Social Security through a tax on employees' wages or salaries.

Pension Plans

A **pension plan** is a retirement program established and funded by the employer and employees. Organizations are not required to offer pension plans to employees, and fewer than half of U.S. workers are covered by them. Small firms offer pension plans less often than do large ones.

Defined-Benefit Pension Plans A "traditional" pension plan, in which the employer makes the contributions and the employee will get a defined amount each month upon retirement, is no longer the norm in the private sector. Through a **defined-benefit plan,** employees are promised a pension amount based on age and service. The employees' contributions are based on actuarial calculations on the *benefits* to be received by the employees after retirement and the *methods* used to determine such benefits. A defined-benefit plan gives employees greater assurance of benefits and greater predictability in the amount of benefits that will be available for retirement.

If the funding in a defined-benefit plan is insufficient, the employer may have to make up the shortfall. Therefore, many employers have dropped defined-benefit plans in favor of defined-contribution plans so that their contribution liabilities are known.[5]

Defined-Contribution Pension Plans In a **defined-contribution plan,** the employer makes an annual payment to an employee's pension account. The key to this plan is the *contribution rate;* employee retirement benefits depend on fixed contributions and employee earnings levels. Profit-sharing plans, employee stock ownership plans (ESOPs), and 401(k) plans are common defined-contribution plans.

Cash Balance Pension Plans Some employers have changed traditional pension plans to cash balance plans, which are hybrids based on ideas from both defined-benefit and defined-contribution plans. One type of plan is a **cash balance plan,** where retirement benefits are based on an accumulation of annual company contributions, expressed as a percentage of pay, plus interest credited each year. With these plans retirement benefits accumulate at the same annual rate until an employee retires. Because cash balance plans spread funding across a worker's entire career, these plans work better for mobile younger workers.

Employee Retirement Income Security Act The widespread criticism of many pension plans led to passage of the Employee Retirement Income Security Act (ERISA) in 1974. The purpose of this law is to regulate private pension plans so that employees who put money into them or depend on a pension for retirement funds actually receive the money when they retire.

ERISA essentially requires many companies to offer retirement plans to all employees if they offer retirement plans to any employees. Accrued benefits must be given to employees when they retire or leave. The act also sets minimum funding requirements, and plans not meeting those requirements are subject to financial penalties imposed by the IRS.

HEALTH-CARE BENEFITS

Employers provide a variety of health-care and medical benefits, usually through insurance coverage. The most common plans cover medical, dental, prescription drug, and vision care expenses for employees and their dependents. Basic health-care insurance to cover both normal and major medical expenses is desired by most employees. Dental insurance is also important to many employees.

Increases in Health Benefits Costs

For several decades, the costs of health care have escalated at a rate well above the rates of inflation and changes in workers' earnings. Since the mid-1990s, employer health-care benefits costs have been increasing significantly faster than inflation or workers' earnings. Estimates are that average health-care benefits costs per employee are over $6,300 a year.[6]

As a result of these large increases, many employers find that dealing with health-care benefits is time-consuming and expensive. This is especially frustrating for employers who have found that many employees seem to take their health benefits for granted.

Retirees Health Benefits Costs A group whose benefits costs are rising is retirees whose former employers still provide health benefit coverage. For instance, at General Motors, on an average there are 2.4 retired employees for every active employee. Increasing the problem at GM is that health-care usage rates for older retirees are significantly higher than current employees. The shocking statistic is that GM has to add $1,400 per vehicle for employee and retiree health-care costs, which costs more than the steel used to build the cars.[7]

Controlling Health-Care Benefits Costs

Employers offering health-care benefits are taking a number of approaches to controlling their costs. The most prominent ones are changing co-payments and employee contributions, using managed care, and switching to consumer-driven health plans.

Changing Co-Payments and Employee Contributions As health insurance costs rise, employers have tried to shift some of those costs to employees. The **co-payment** strategy requires employees to pay a portion of the cost of insurance premiums, medical care, and prescription drugs.

Using Managed Care Several other types of programs attempt to reduce health-care costs paid by employers. **Managed care** consists of approaches that monitor and reduce medical costs through restrictions and market system alternatives. Managed care plans emphasize primary and preventive care, the use of specific providers who will charge lower prices, restrictions on certain kinds of treatment, and prices negotiated with hospitals and physicians.

Consumer-Driven Health Plans Many employers are turning to employee-focused health benefits plans. The most prominent is a **consumer-driven health (CDH) plan,** which provides financial contributions to employees to cover their own health-related expenses.

In these plans, which are also called *defined-contribution health plans,* an employer places a set amount into each employee's account and identifies a number of health-care alternatives that are available. Then, individual employees select from those health-care alternatives and pay for them from their accounts.

CDH plans can be coupled with *health flexible spending accounts* (*health reimbursement arrangements, medical savings accounts,* and *health savings accounts*). There are two advantages to such plans for employers. One is that more of the increases in health-care benefits are shifted to employees, because the employer contributions need not increase as fast as health-care costs. Second, the focus of controlling health-care usage falls on employees, who may have to choose when to use and not use health-care benefits.

As would be expected, many employees are skeptical about or even hostile to employer efforts to control health benefits costs. Surveys of employees have found that they are more dissatisfied with changes to their health benefits than with the moderation of base pay increases. In fact, over half of the employees in one survey said that they would forgo any pay increase to keep their health benefits unchanged.[8]

Health-Care Legislation

The importance of health-care benefits to employers and employees has led to a variety of federal and state laws. Some laws have been enacted to provide protection for employees who leave their employers, either voluntarily or involuntarily. To date, the two most important ones are COBRA and HIPAA.

COBRA Provisions The Consolidated Omnibus Budget Reconciliation Act (COBRA) requires that most employers (except churches and the federal government) with 20 or more employees offer extended health-care coverage to certain groups, as follows:

▶ Employees who voluntarily quit
▶ Widowed or divorced spouses and dependent children of former or current employees
▶ Retirees and their spouses whose health-care coverage ends

Employers must notify eligible employees and/or their spouses and qualified dependents within 60 days after the employees quit, die, get divorced, or otherwise change their status.

HIPAA Provisions The Health Insurance Portability and Accountability Act (HIPAA) of 1996 allows employees to switch their health insurance plans when they change employers, and to get new health coverage with the new company regardless of preexisting health conditions. The legislation also prohibits group insurance plans from dropping coverage for a sick employee, and requires them to make individual coverage available to people who leave group plans.

One of the greatest impacts of HIPAA comes from its provisions on the privacy of employee medical records. These provisions require employers to provide privacy notices to employees. They also regulate the disclosure of protected health information without authorization.

FINANCIAL BENEFITS

Employers may offer workers a wide range of special benefits that provide financial support to employees: financial services, relocation assistance, insurance benefits (in addition to health insurance), educational assistance, and others. Employers find that such benefits can be useful in attracting and retaining employees. Workers like receiving the following benefits, which often are not taxed as income:

► Financial Services
► Relocation Assistance
► Insurance Benefits
► Educational Assistance

FAMILY-ORIENTED BENEFITS

The composition of families in the United States has changed significantly in the past few decades. The number of traditional families, in which the man went to work and the woman stayed home to raise children, has declined significantly, while the percentage of two-worker families has more than doubled. The growth in dual-career couples, single-parent households, and work demands on many workers have increased the emphasis some employers are placing on family-oriented benefits. As mentioned in earlier chapters, balancing family and work demands presents a major challenge to many workers at all levels of organizations. Therefore, employers have established a variety of family-oriented benefits. Since 1993, employers have also been required to provide certain benefits to comply with the Family and Medical Leave Act.

Family and Medical Leave Act

The Family and Medical Leave Act (FMLA) covers all federal, state, and private employers with 50 or more employees who live within 75 miles of the workplace. Only employees who have worked at least 12 months and 1,250 hours in the previous year are eligible for leave under the FMLA.

FMLA Leave Provisions The law requires that employers allow eligible employees to take a total of 12 weeks' leave during any 12-month period for one or more of three situations. Those situations are:

► Birth, adoption, or foster care placement of a child
► Caring for a spouse, a child, or a parent with a serious health condition
► Serious health condition of the employee

Results of the FMLA Since the passage of the act, several factors have become apparent. First, a significant percentage of employees have been taking family and medical leave.

Second, many employers have not paid enough attention to the law. Some employers are denying leave or failing to reinstate workers after leave is completed. Consequently, numerous lawsuits have resulted, many of which are lost by employers. Many employers' problems with the FMLA occur because of the variety of circumstances in which employees may request and use family leave.

Benefits for Domestic Partners

As lifestyles change in the United States, employers are being confronted with requests for benefits by employees who are not married but have close personal relationships with others. The terms often used to refer to individuals with such arrangements are *domestic partners* or *spousal equivalents*. The employees who are submitting these requests are: (1) unmarried employees who are living with individuals of the opposite sex and (2) gay and lesbian employees who have partners. In 13 states and 150 cities, laws have been enacted to require employers to grant domestic partners the same benefits rights that they give to traditional married couples.[9]

TIME-OFF AND OTHER MISCELLANEOUS BENEFITS

Time-off benefits represent an estimated 5%–13% of total compensation. Employers give employees paid time off in a variety of circumstances. Paid lunch breaks and rest periods, holidays, and vacations are common. But time off is given for a number of other purposes as follows:

► Holiday Pay
► Vacation Pay
► Leave of Absence
► Paid-Time-Off Plans

Employers also offer a wide variety of miscellaneous benefits. Some of the benefits are voluntary, meaning that employees can participate in them and pay for the costs themselves, often at group discount rates. Others are unique to employers and are provided at little or no cost to employees.

BENEFITS ADMINISTRATION

With the myriad of benefits and regulations, it is easy to see why many organizations must make coordinated efforts to administer benefits programs.

Benefits Communication

Employees generally do not know much about the values and costs associated with the benefits they receive from employers, so benefits communication and benefits satisfaction are linked. Consequently, many employers have instituted special benefits communication systems to inform employees about the value of the benefits they provide.

Benefits Statements Some employers also give each employee a "personal statement of benefits" that translates benefits into dollar amounts. Federal regulations require that employees receive an annual pension-reporting statement, which also can be included in the personal statement. Employers hope that by educating employees about their benefits and the costs, they can better manage expenditures and can give employees a better appreciation of the value of employers' payments.

HR Technology and Benefits

The spread of HR technology, particularly Internet-based systems, has significantly changed the benefits administration time and activities for HR staff members. Internet-based systems are being used to communicate benefits information, conduct employee benefits surveys, and facilitate other benefits communications.

Flexible Benefits

As part of both benefits design and administration many employers have flexible benefits plans that offer employees choices. A **flexible benefits plan,** sometimes called a *flex plan* or *cafeteria plan,* allows employees to select the benefits they prefer from groups of benefits established by the employer. By having a variety of "dishes," or benefits, available, each employee can select an individual combination of benefits within some overall limits.

Problems with Flexible Plans A problem with flexibility in benefits choice is that an *inappropriate benefits package* may be chosen by an employee. A young construction worker may not choose a disability benefit; however, if he or she is injured, the family may suffer financial hardship. Part of this problem can be overcome by requiring employees to select a core set of benefits (life, health, and disability insurance) and then offering options on other benefits.

Also, because many flexible plans have become so complex, they require more administrative time and information systems to track the different choices made by employees. Despite all these disadvantages, flex plans will likely continue to grow in popularity.

NOTES

1. Dorren Remmen, "Performance Pays Off," *Strategic Finance,* March 2003, 27–32.
2. Tom Wilson and Harold N. Altmansberger, "Taking Variable Pay to a New Level," *Workspan,* December 2003, 44–47.
3. Edward E. Lawler III, "Pay Practices in *Fortune* 1000 Corporations," *WorldatWork Journal,* Fourth Quarter 2003, 45–54.
4. U.S. Bureau of Labor Statistics, *http://www.bls.gov.*
5. Maureen Minehan, "Employer-Sponsored Pensions," *Workplace Visions,* 1 (2003).
6. *http://www.uschamber.com* or *http://www.uschamber.com/research*
7. "Retiree Health-Care Costs Climb to $63.4 Billion at GM," *Omaha World-Herald,* March 12, 2004, B1.
8. "Majority Says a Significant Reduction in Health Benefits Is Worse than No Pay Increase," *Wall Street Journal,* October 24, 2003, p. B1.
9. Kelly Blassingame, "Domestic Partner Mandate Complicates Decision Making," *Employee Benefit News,* March 2004, 1, 15.

INTERNET RESOURCES

HR Guide—Compensation This Web site discusses incentives in detail. **http://www.hr-guide. com**

Synygy Inc. At this Web site, the largest provider of software and services for managing variable pay plans provides free case studies and publications. **http://www.synygy.com**

SUGGESTED READINGS

Handbook of Employee Benefits, McGraw-Hill, 2005.

Managing Benefits Plans, IOMA, 2003.

McGladrey and Pullen, LLP, *Mandated Benefits,* Aspen, 2005.

Scott S. Roderick, *Incentive Compensation and Employee Ownership*, The National Center for Employee Ownership, 2004.

Chapter 9

Employee Relations

Today, employers are expected to provide work environments that are safe, secure, and healthy. However, at one time, employers viewed accidents and occupational diseases as unavoidable by-products of work. This idea may still be prevalent in some less-developed countries. Fortunately, in the United States and most developed nations, it has been replaced with the concept of using prevention and control to minimize or eliminate risks in workplaces.

Further, employee rights, the policies established for HR in an organization, and discipline to enforce those policies are critical elements for employee relations.

Managerial Perspectives on HR

1. Why is controlling workers' compensation costs important?

2. Explain the essential relationships among employee rights, HR policies, and employee discipline.

3. Consider the following: "Even though restructuring employees' free speech rights at work is permissible—there might be consequences for doing that."

HEALTH, SAFETY, AND SECURITY

The terms *health, safety,* and *security* are closely related. The broader and somewhat more nebulous term is **health,** which refers to a general state of physical, mental, and emotional well-being. A healthy person is free from illness, injury, or mental and emotional problems that impair normal human activity. Health management practices in organizations strive to maintain the overall well-being of individuals.

Typically, **safety** refers to a condition in which the physical well-being of people is protected. The main purpose of effective safety programs in organizations is to prevent work-related injuries and accidents. The purpose of **security** is protecting employees and organizational facilities. With the growth of workplace violence, security at work has become an even greater concern for employers and employees alike.

About 4.7 million nonfatal injuries and illnesses occur at work annually, which gives an average injury rate of 5.3 cases per 100 employees. Specific rates vary depending on the industry, job, etc., with 1.7 cases per 100 employees in the finance industry and 7.2 cases per 100 in manufacturing.[1]

The three major causes of injury (overextending, falling, and bodily reaction) were responsible for over half of the direct costs of injury. Accident *costs* have gone up faster than inflation because of the rapid increase in medical costs, even though the number of accidents has been decreasing for some time. The main safety enforcement agency of the federal government, the Occupational Safety and Health Administration (OSHA), gave 8% more citations (83,760) to employers in one recent year and focused on repeat offenders, while the *rate* of injuries and fatalities at work reached the lowest point ever.[2]

LEGAL REQUIREMENTS FOR SAFETY AND HEALTH

Employers must comply with a variety of federal and state laws when developing and maintaining healthy, safe, and secure workforces and working environments. Three major legal areas are workers' compensation legislation, the Americans with Disabilities Act, and child labor laws.

Workers' Cosmpensation.

First passed in the early 1900s, workers' compensation laws in some form are on the books in all states today. Under these laws, employers contribute to an insurance fund to compensate employees for injuries received while on the job. Premiums paid reflect the accident rates of the employers, with employers that have higher incident rates being assessed higher premiums.

Workers' compensation costs have increased for many employers and have become a major issue in many states. These costs represent from 2%–10% of payroll for most employers. The major contributors to the increases have been higher medical costs and litigation expenses.

The Family and Medical Leave Act (FMLA) affects workers' compensation as well. Because the FMLA allows eligible employees to take up to 12 weeks of leave for their serious health conditions, injured employees may ask to use that leave time in addition to the leave time allowed under workers' comp, even if it is unpaid. Some employers have policies that state that FMLA runs concurrently with any workers' comp leave.

Americans with Disabilities Act and Safety Issues

Employers sometimes try to return injured workers to "light-duty" work in order to reduce workers' compensation costs. However, under the Americans with Disabilities Act, when making accommodations for injured employees through light-duty work, employers may undercut what are really essential job functions. Also, making such accommodations for injured employees for a period of time may require employers to make similar accommodations for job applicants with disabilities.

Child Labor Laws

Safety concerns are reflected in restrictions affecting younger workers, especially those under the age of 18. Child labor laws, found in Section XII of the Fair Labor Standards Act (FLSA), set the minimum age for most employment at 16 years. For "hazardous" occupations, 18 years is the minimum.

In addition to complying with workers' compensation, the Americans with Disabilities Act (ADA), and child labor laws, most employers must comply with the Occupational Safety and Health Act of 1970. This act has had a tremendous impact on the workplace.

OCCUPATIONAL SAFETY AND HEALTH ACT

The Occupational Safety and Health Act of 1970 was passed "to assure so far as possible every working man or woman in the Nation safe and healthful working conditions and to preserve our human resources." Every employer that is engaged in commerce and has one or more employees is covered by the act. Farmers having fewer than 10 employees are exempt. Employers in specific industries, such as coal mining, are covered under other health and safety acts. Federal, state, and local governments are covered by separate statutes and provisions.

OSHA Enforcement Standards

To implement OSHA, specific standards were established regulating equipment and working environments. National standards developed by engineering and quality control groups are often used. OSHA rules and standards are frequently complicated and technical. Small-business owners and managers who do not have specialists on their staffs may find the standards difficult to read and understand. In addition, the presence of many minor standards has hurt the credibility of OSHA.

A number of provisions have been recognized as key to employers' efforts to comply with OSHA. Two basic ones are as follows:

▶ *General duty:* The act requires that the employer has a "general duty" to provide safe and healthy working conditions, even in areas where OSHA standards have not been set. Employers who know or reasonably should know of unsafe or unhealthy conditions can be cited for violating the general duty clause.
▶ *Notification and posters:* Employers are required to inform their employees of safety and health standards established by OSHA. Also, OSHA posters must be displayed in prominent locations in workplaces.

Hazard Communication OSHA has enforcement responsibilities for the federal Hazard Communication standard, which requires manufacturers, importers, distributors, and users of hazardous chemicals to evaluate, classify, and label these substances. Employers also must make available to employees, their representatives, and health professionals information about hazardous substances. This information is contained in material safety data sheets (MSDSs), which must be kept readily accessible to those who work with chemicals and other substances. The MSDSs also indicate antidotes or actions to be taken should someone come in contact with the substances.

Bloodborne Pathogens OSHA has issued a standard regarding exposure to hepatitis B virus (HBV), human immunodeficiency virus (HIV), and other bloodborne pathogens. This regulation was developed to protect employees who regularly are exposed to blood and other such substances from contracting AIDS and other serious diseases. Obviously, health-care laboratory workers, nurses, and medical technicians are at greatest risk. However, all employers covered by OSHA regulations must comply in workplaces where cuts and abrasions are common.

Personal Protective Equipment One goal of OSHA has been to develop standards for personal protective equipment (PPE). These standards require that employers analyze job hazards, provide adequate PPE to employees in hazardous jobs, and train employees in the use of PPE items. Common PPE items include safety glasses, hard hats, and safety shoes. If the work environment presents hazards or if employees might have contact with hazardous chemicals and substances on the job, then employers are required to provide PPE to all those employees.

Ergonomics and OSHA

Ergonomics is the study and design of the work environment to address physiological and physical demands on individuals. In a work setting, ergonomic studies look at such factors as fatigue, lighting, tools, equipment layout, and placement of controls.

For a number of years, OSHA focused on the large number of work-related injuries due to repetitive stress, repetitive motion, cumulative trauma disorders, carpal tunnel syndrome, and other causes. **Cumulative trauma disorders (CTDs)** are muscle and skeletal injuries that occur when workers repetitively use the same muscles to perform tasks.

OSHA Recordkeeping Requirements

OSHA has established a standard national system for recording occupational injuries, accidents, and fatalities. Employers are generally required to maintain a detailed annual record of the various types of accidents, for inspection by OSHA representatives and for submission to the agency. Employers that have had good safety records in previous years and those with fewer than 10 employees are not required to keep detailed records. Because of revisions effective in 2002, many organizations must complete OSHA Form 300 to report workshop accidents and injuries. These organizations include firms having frequent hospitalizations, injuries, illnesses, or work-related deaths, and firms in a labor statistics survey conducted by OSHA each year.

OSHA Inspections

The Occupational Safety and Health Act provides for on-the-spot inspections by OSHA representatives, called compliance officers or inspectors. In *Marshall v. Barlow's, Inc.,* the U.S. Supreme Court has held that safety inspectors must produce a search warrant if an employer refuses to allow an inspector into the plant voluntarily. The Court also ruled that an inspector does not have to show probable cause to obtain a search warrant. A warrant can easily be obtained if a search is part of a general enforcement plan.[3]

Critique of OSHA Inspection Efforts

OSHA has been criticized on several fronts. Because the agency has so many work sites to inspect, many employers have only a relatively small chance of being inspected. Some suggest that many employers pay little attention to OSHA enforcement efforts for this reason. Labor unions and others have criticized OSHA and Congress for not providing enough inspectors. For instance, it is common to find that many of the work sites at which workers suffered severe injuries or deaths had not been inspected in the previous five years.

Employers, especially smaller ones, continue to complain about the complexity of complying with OSHA standards and the costs associated with penalties and with making changes required to remedy problem areas. Very small employers point out that according to statistics from OSHA, their businesses already have significantly lower work-related injury and illness rates than larger ones. Larger firms can afford to hire safety and health specialists and establish more proactive programs.

SAFETY MANAGEMENT

Well-designed and well-managed safety programs can pay dividends in reduced accidents and associated costs, such as workers' compensation and possible fines. Further, accidents and other safety concerns usually decline as a result of management efforts emphasizing safety. Often, the difference between firms with good safety performance and firms that OSHA has targeted as being well below the industry average is that the former have effective safety management programs.

Successful safety management is not a mystery. The topic has been researched extensively. A summary of what is known about managing to minimize accidents includes discussion of these issues:

▶ Organizational commitment
▶ Policies, discipline, and recordkeeping
▶ Training and communication

FIGURE 9.1   Approaches to Effective Safety Management

▶ Participation (safety committees)

▶ Inspection, investigation, and evaluation

Organizational Commitment and a Safety Culture

Three approaches are used by employers in managing safety. Figure 9.1 shows the organizational, engineering, and individual approaches and their components. Successful programs may use all three in dealing with safety issues.

At the heart of safety management is an organizational commitment to a comprehensive safety effort. This effort should be coordinated from the top level of management to include all members of the organization. It should also be reflected in managerial actions.

Safety Policies, Discipline, and Recordkeeping

Designing safety policies and rules and disciplining violators are important components of safety efforts. Frequently reinforcing the need for safe behavior and frequently supplying feedback on positive safety practices are also effective ways of improving worker safety. Such efforts must involve employees, supervisors, managers, safety specialists, and HR staff members.

For policies about safety to be effective, good recordkeeping about accidents, causes, and other details is necessary. Without records, an employer cannot benchmark its safety performance against other employers and may not realize there is a problem.

Safety Training and Communication

Good safety training reduces accidents. Supervisors should receive the training first, and then employees should receive it as well, because untrained workers are more likely to have accidents. Safety training can be done in various ways. Regular sessions with supervisors, managers, and employees are often coordinated by HR staff members. Communication of safety procedures, reasons why accidents occurred, and what to do in an emergency is critical. Without effective communication about safety, training is insufficient.

Safety Committees

Employees frequently participate in safety planning through safety committees, often composed of workers from a variety of levels and departments. A safety committee generally meets at regularly scheduled times, has specific responsibilities for conducting safety reviews, and makes recommendations for changes necessary to avoid future accidents. Usually, at least one member of the committee comes from the HR department.

Inspection, Investigation, and Evaluation

It is not necessary to wait for an OSHA inspector to check the work area for safety hazards. Inspections may be done by a safety committee or by a safety coordinator. They should be done regularly, and problem areas should be addressed immediately, to keep work productivity at the highest possible levels. Also, OSHA inspects organizations with above-average rates of lost workdays more frequently.

When accidents occur, they should be investigated by the employer's safety committee or safety coordinator. In investigating the scene of an accident, the inspector needs to determine which physical and environmental conditions contributed to the accident. Investigation at the scene should be done as soon as possible after an accident to ensure that the conditions under which the accident occurred have not changed significantly.

EMPLOYEE HEALTH

Employee health problems are varied—and somewhat inevitable. They can range from minor illnesses such as colds to serious illnesses related to the jobs performed. Some employees have emotional health problems; others have alcohol or drug problems. Some problems are chronic; others are transitory. All may affect organizational operations and individual employee productivity.

Workplace Health Issues

Employers face a variety of workplace health issues. Some key concerns associated are employee substance abuse, emotional/mental health, workplace air quality, and smoking at work.

Substance Abuse Use of illicit substances or misuse of controlled substances, alcohol, or other drugs is called **substance abuse.** The millions of substance abusers in the workforce cost global employers billions of dollars annually. In the United States, the incidence of substance abuse is greatest among white men ages 19–23. At work, it is higher among men than women and higher among whites than other groups.

Most large companies test applicants and employees for drug use. Many small companies do not. As a result, small companies may become havens for drug users—places they can get a job. The most common tests for drug use are urinalysis, radioimmunoassay of hair, and fitness-for-duty testing. *Urinalysis* is used most frequently. It requires a urine sample, which must be tested at a lab. Despite concerns about sample switching and the ability of the test to detect drug use only over the past few days, urinalysis is generally accurate and well accepted.

Drug-Free Workplace Act of 1988 The U.S. Supreme Court has ruled that certain drug-testing plans do not violate the Constitution. Private-employer programs are governed mainly by state laws, which can be a confusing hodgepodge. The Drug-Free Workplace Act of 1988 requires government contractors to take steps to eliminate employee drug use. Failure to do so can lead to contract termination. Tobacco and alcohol do not qualify as controlled substances under the act, and off-the-job drug use is not included. Additionally, the U.S. Department of Transportation (DOT) requires regular testing of truck and bus drivers, train crews, mass-transit employees, airline pilots and mechanics, pipeline workers, and licensed sailors.

The Americans with Disabilities Act (ADA) affects how management can handle substance abuse cases. Current users of illegal drugs are specifically excluded from the definition of *disabled* under the act. However, those addicted to legal substances (alcohol, for example) and prescription drugs are considered disabled under the ADA. Also, recovering substance abusers are considered disabled under the ADA.

Emotional/Mental Health Many individuals today are facing work, family, and personal life pressures. A variety of emotional/mental health issues arise at work that must be addressed by employers. It is important to note that emotional/mental illnesses such as schizophrenia and depression are considered disabilities under the ADA. Employers should be cautious when using disciplinary policies if employees diagnosed with such illnesses have work-related problems.

Smoking at Work Arguments and rebuttals characterize the smoking-at-work controversy, and statistics abound. A multitude of state and local laws deal with smoking in the workplace and in public places. In response to health studies, complaints by nonsmokers, and state laws, many employers have instituted no-smoking policies throughout their workplaces.

Health Promotion

Employers concerned about maintaining a healthy workforce must move beyond simply providing healthy working conditions and begin promoting employee health and wellness in other ways. **Health promotion** is a supportive approach of facilitating and encouraging healthy actions and lifestyles among employees. Health promotion efforts can range from providing information and increasing employee awareness of health issues, to creating an organizational culture supportive of employee health enhancements. Two key means are wellness programs and employee assistance programs.

SECURITY CONCERNS AT WORK

Traditionally, when employers have addressed worker health, safety, and security, they have been concerned about reducing workplace accidents, improving workers' safety practices, and reducing health hazards at work. Over the past decade, providing security for employees has grown in importance. Top security concerns at work are as follows:

► Workplace violence
► Internet/intranet security
► Business interruption/disaster recovery
► Fraud/white-collar crime
► Employee selection/screening concerns

Workplace Violence

The National Institute for Occupational Safety and Health (NIOSH) estimates that 10–15 workplace homicides occur every week. It also estimates that an additional 1 million people are attacked at work each year.[4] About 70% of workplace fatalities involve attacks against workers such as police officers, taxi drivers, and convenience store clerks. Often, these deaths occur during armed robbery attempts.

There are a number of warning signs and characteristics of a potentially violent person at work. Individuals who have committed the most violent acts have had the relatively common profile depicted in Figure 9.2. A person with some of these signs may cope for years until a trauma pushes the individual over the edge. A profound humiliation or rejection, the end of a marriage, the loss of a lawsuit, or termination from a job may make a difficult employee turn violent.

Management of Workplace Violence The increase in workplace violence has led many employers to develop policies and practices for preventing and responding to workplace violence. As a first step, employers need to conduct a risk assessment of the organization and its employees. Unfortunately, few employers have conducted such a study. After completing a study, an organization can establish HR policies to identify how workplace violence is to be dealt with in conjunction with disciplinary actions and referrals to employee assistance programs.

FIGURE 9.2 Profile of a Potentially Violent Employee

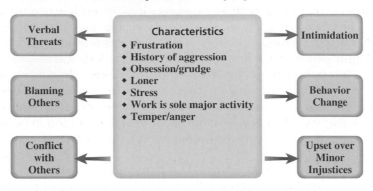

Security Management

An overall approach to security management is needed to address a wide range of issues, including workplace violence. Often, HR managers have responsibility for security programs, or they work closely with security managers or consultants to address employee security issues.

In a **security audit,** HR staff conduct a comprehensive review of organizational security. Sometimes called a *vulnerability analysis,* such an audit uses managers inside the organization (such as the HR manager and the facilities manager) and outsiders (such as security consultants, police officers, fire officials, and computer security experts) to assess security issues.

Employee Screening and Selection

A key facet of providing security is screening job applicants. Regulations somewhat limit what can be done, particularly regarding the use of psychological tests and checking of references. However, firms that do not screen employees adequately may be subject to liability if an employee commits crimes later. For instance, an individual with a criminal record for assault was hired by a firm to maintain sound equipment in clients' homes. The employee used a passkey to enter a home and assault the owner, and the employer was ruled liable. Of course, when selecting employees, employers must be careful to use only valid, job-related screening means and to avoid violating federal EEO laws and the Americans with Disabilities Act.

RIGHTS AND RESPONSIBILITIES ISSUES

There are three related and important issues in managing human resources: employee rights, HR policies and rules, and discipline. These areas may seem separate, but they definitely are not. The policies and rules that an organization enacts help to define employees' rights at that employer, as well as constrain those rights (sometimes inappropriately or illegally). Similarly, discipline for those who fail to follow policies and rules is often seen as a fundamental right of employers. Employees who feel that their employers have taken inappropriate action can challenge that action—both inside and outside the organization—using an internal dispute resolution process or through a variety of external legal means.

Rights generally do not exist in the abstract. Instead, they exist only when someone is successful in demanding their application. **Rights** are powers, privileges, or interests that belong to a person by law, nature, or tradition. Of course, defining a right presents considerable potential for disagreement. For example, does an employee have a right to privacy of communication in personal matters when using the employer's computer on company time? Moreover, *legal rights* may or may not correspond to certain *moral rights,* and the reverse is true as well—a situation that opens "rights" up to controversy and lawsuits.

Rights are offset by **responsibilities,** which are obligations to perform certain tasks and duties. Employment is a reciprocal relationship (both sides have rights and obligations). For example, if an employee has the right to a safe working environment, then the employer must have an obligation to provide a safe workplace. If the employer has a right to expect uninterrupted, high-quality work from the employee, then the worker has the responsibility to be on the job and to meet job performance standards. The reciprocal nature of rights and responsibilities suggests that both parties to an employment relationship should regard the other as having rights and should treat the other with respect.

Employees' **statutory rights** are the result of specific laws or statutes passed by federal, state, or local governments. Various federal, state, and local laws have granted employees certain rights at work, such as equal employment opportunity, collective bargaining, and workplace safety. These laws and their interpretations also have been the subjects of a considerable number of court cases.

An employee's **contractual rights** are based on a specific contract with an employer. For instance, a union and an employer may agree on a labor contract that specifies certain terms, conditions, and rights that employees represented by the union have with the employer.

Employment Contracts

A formal **employment contract** is an agreement that outlines the details of employment. Written employment contracts are often very detailed. Traditionally, employment contracts have been used mostly for executives and senior managers, but the use of employment contracts is filtering down the organization to include highly specialized professional and technical employees who have scarce skills.

Implied Contracts

The idea that a contract (even an implied or unwritten one) exists between individuals and their employers affects the employment relationship. The rights and responsibilities of the employee may be spelled out in a job description, in an employment contract, in HR policies, or in a handbook, but often are not. The rights and responsibilities of the employee may also exist *only* as unwritten employer expectations about what is acceptable behavior or performance on the part of the employee. For instance, a number of court decisions have held that if an employer hires someone for an indefinite period or promises job security, the employer has created an implied contract. Such promises establish employee expectations, especially if there has been a long-term business relationship. When the employer fails to follow up on the implied promises, the employee may pursue remedies in court. Numerous federal and state court decisions have held that such implied promises, especially when contained in an employee handbook, constitute a contract between an employer and its employees, even without a signed document.

RIGHTS AFFECTING THE EMPLOYMENT RELATIONSHIP

As employees increasingly regard themselves as free agents in the workplace—and as the power of unions declines—the struggle between individual employee and employer rights is heightening. Several concepts from law and psychology influence the employment relationship: employment-at-will, just cause, due process, and distributive and procedural justice.

Employment-at-Will

Employment-at-will (EAW) is a common-law doctrine stating that employers have the right to hire, fire, demote, or promote whomever they choose, unless there is a law or a contract to the contrary. Conversely, employees can quit whenever they want and go to another job under the same constraints. An employment-at-will statement usually contains wording such as the following:

> *This handbook is not a contract, express or implied, guaranteeing employment for any specific duration. Although we hope that your employment relationship with us will be long-term, either you or the Employer may terminate this relationship at any time, for any reason, with or without cause or notice.*

Wrongful Discharge

Employers who run afoul of EAW restrictions may be guilty of **wrongful discharge,** which is the termination of an individual's employment for reasons that are illegal or improper. Some state courts have recognized certain non-statutory grounds for wrongful-discharge suits. Additionally, courts generally have held that unionized workers cannot pursue EAW actions as at-will employees because they are covered by the grievance arbitration process.

Employers should take several precautions to reduce wrongful discharge liabilities. Having a well-written employee handbook, training managers, and maintaining adequate documentation are key. Figure 9.3 offers suggestions for preparing a defense against wrongful-discharge lawsuits.

FIGURE 9.3   Keys for Preparing a Defense Against Wrongful Discharge: The "Paper Trail"

Performance Appraisal
Make sure performance appraisals give an accurate picture of the person's performance.

Written Records
Maintain written records on behaviors leading to dismissal.

Written Warning
Warn employee in writing before dismissal.

Group Involvement
Involve more than one person in the termination decision.

Grounds for Dismissal
Put grounds for dismissal in writing.

Closely related to wrongful discharge is **constructive discharge,** which is deliberately making conditions intolerable to get an employee to quit. Under normal circumstances, an employee who resigns rather than being dismissed cannot later collect damages for violation of legal rights. An exception to this rule occurs when the courts find that the working conditions were made so intolerable as to *force* a reasonable employee to resign. Then, the resignation is considered a discharge.

Alternative Dispute Resolution

Disputes between management and employees over different work issues are normal and inevitable. How the parties resolve their disputes becomes important. **Arbitration** is a process that uses a neutral third party to make a decision, thereby eliminating the necessity of using the court system.

Some employers allow their employees to appeal disciplinary actions to an internal committee of employees. This panel reviews the actions and makes recommendations or decisions. Panel members are specially trained volunteers who sign confidentiality agreements, after which the company empowers them to hear appeals.

BALANCING EMPLOYER SECURITY CONCERNS AND EMPLOYEE RIGHTS

The **right to privacy** is defined in legal terms as an individual's freedom from unauthorized and unreasonable intrusion into personal affairs. Although the right to privacy is not specifically identified in the U.S. Constitution, a number of past Supreme Court cases have established that such a right must be considered.

Also, several states have enacted right-to-privacy statutes. HR policies and priorities in organizations are specifically affected by such issues as access to employee records, employees' freedom of speech, workplace monitoring, employer investigations, and substance abuse and drug testing.

Employees' Free Speech Rights

The right of individuals to freedom of speech is protected by the U.S. Constitution. However, that freedom is *not* an unrestricted one in the workplace. Three areas in which employees' freedom of speech have collided with employers' restrictions are controversial views, whistle-blowing, and monitoring of e-mail and voice mail.

Questions of free speech arise over the right of employees to advocate controversial viewpoints at work. Numerous examples can be cited. For instance: Can an employee of a tobacco company join in antismoking demonstrations outside of work? In situations such as these, employers must follow due process procedures and demonstrate that disciplinary actions taken against employees can be justified by job-related reasons.

Whistle-Blowing Individuals who report real or perceived wrongs committed by their employers are called **whistle-blowers.** The reasons why people report actions that they question vary, and are often individual in nature. Many well-known whistle-blowing incidents have occurred in the past several years. Whistle-blowers are less likely to lose their jobs in public employment than in private employment, because most civil service systems follow rules protecting whistle-blowers. However, no comprehensive whistle-blowing law fully protects the right to free speech of both public and private employees.

Monitoring of E-mail and Voice Mail Employers increasingly have a right to monitor what is said and transmitted through their e-mail and voice-mail systems, despite employees' concerns about free speech. Advances in information and telecommunications technology have become a major issue for employers regarding employee privacy.[5] The use of e-mail and voice mail increases every day, along with employers' liability if they improperly monitor or inspect employees' electronic communications. Many employers have specialized software that can retrieve deleted e-mail, and even record each keystroke made on their computers.

There are recommended actions for employers to take when monitoring e-mail and voice mail. These actions include creating an *electronic communications policy* and getting employees to sign a *permission form.* With these steps in place, employers should monitor only for business purposes and should strictly enforce the policy.

Workplace Monitoring

The monitoring of e-mail and voice mail is only one illustration of how employers watch the workplace. In the United States, the right of protection from unreasonable search and seizure protects an individual against activities of the government only. Thus, employees of both private sector and governmental employers can be monitored, observed, and searched at work by representatives of the employer. Several court decisions have reaffirmed the principle that both private-sector and government employers may search desks, files, lockers, and computer files without search warrants if they believe that work rules were violated.[6]

Monitoring Employee Performance Employee activity may be monitored to measure performance, ensure performance quality and customer service, check for theft, or enforce company rules or laws. The common concerns in a monitored workplace usually center not on whether or not monitoring should be used, but on how it should be conducted, how the information should be used, and how feedback should be communicated to employees.

At a minimum, employers should obtain a signed employee consent form that indicates that performance will be monitored regularly and phone calls will be taped regularly. Also, it is recommended that employers provide employees with feedback on monitoring results to help employees improve their performance and to commend them for good performance.

Conducting Video Surveillance at Work Numerous employers have installed video surveillance systems in workplaces. Some employers use these systems to ensure employee security, such as in parking lots, garages, and dimly lit exterior areas. Other employers have installed them on retail sales floors and in production areas, parts and inventory rooms, and lobbies. When video surveillance is extended into employee restrooms, changing rooms, and other more private areas, employer rights and employee privacy collide. As with other forms of monitoring, it is important that employers develop a video surveillance policy, inform employees about the policy, perform the surveillance only for legitimate business purposes, and strictly limit those who view the surveillance results.

Honesty and Polygraph Tests Pencil-and-paper honesty tests are alternatives to polygraph testing. These tests are widely used, particularly in the retail industry and in other selected industries, and more than two dozen variations of them are available. However, their use has been challenged successfully in some court decisions.

Conducting Work-Related Investigations Workplace investigations are frequently conducted using technology. Technological advances allow employers to review e-mails, access computer logs, conduct video surveillance, and use other investigative tactics. When using audiotaping, wiretapping, and other electronic methods, care should be taken to avoid violating privacy and legal regulations.

Workplace investigations can be conducted internally or externally. Often, HR staff and company security personnel lead internal investigations. Until recently, the use of outside investigators—the police, private investigators, attorneys, or others—was restricted by the Fair Credit Reporting Act. However, passage of the Fair and Accurate Credit Transactions (FACT) Act changed the situation. Under FACT, employers can hire outside investigators without first notifying the individuals under investigation or getting their permission.[7]

HR POLICIES, PROCEDURES, AND RULES

HR policies, procedures, and rules greatly affect employee rights (just discussed) and discipline (discussed next). Where there is a choice among actions, **policies** act as general guidelines that focus organizational actions. Policies are general in nature, whereas procedures and rules are specific to the situation. The important role of policies requires that they be reviewed regularly.

Procedures provide customary methods of handling activities and are more specific than policies. For example, a policy may state that employees will be given vacations according to years of service, and a procedure establishes a specific method for authorizing vacation time without disrupting work.

Rules are specific guidelines that regulate and restrict the behavior of individuals. They are similar to procedures in that they guide action and typically allow no discretion in their application. Rules reflect a management decision that action be taken—or not taken—in a given situation, and they provide more specific behavioral guidelines than do policies.

Employee Handbooks

Employee handbooks give employees a reference source for company policies and rules and can be a positive tool for effective management of human resources. Even small organizations can prepare handbooks relatively easily using available computer software. When preparing handbooks, management should consider legal issues, readability, and use.

Legal Review of Language   As mentioned earlier, there is a current trend of using employee handbooks against employers in lawsuits charging a broken "implied" contract. This tendency should not eliminate the use of employee handbooks as a way of communicating policies to employees. In fact, not having an employee handbook with HR policies spelled out can leave an organization open to costly litigation and out-of-court settlements. A more sensible approach is to first develop sound HR policies and employee handbooks to communicate them, and then have legal counsel review the language contained in them.

Employee Discipline

The earlier discussion about employee rights provides an appropriate introduction to the topic of employee discipline, because employee rights often are a key issue in disciplinary cases. **Discipline** is a form of training that enforces organizational rules. Those most often affected by the discipline systems are problem employees.

The disciplinary system can be viewed as an application of behavior modification to problem or unproductive employees. The best discipline is clearly self-discipline. Most people can usually be counted on to do their jobs effectively when they understand what is required at work. Yet some find that the prospect of external discipline helps their self-discipline. One approach is use of a positive discipline approach.

Positive Discipline Approach The positive discipline approach builds on the philosophy that violations are actions that can usually be corrected constructively without penalty. In this approach, managers focus on using fact-finding and guidance to encourage desirable behaviors, rather than using penalties to discourage undesirable behaviors.

Progressive Discipline Approach Progressive discipline incorporates steps that become progressively more stringent and are designed to change the employee's inappropriate behavior. Figure 9.4 shows a typical progressive discipline process; most progressive discipline procedures use verbal and written reprimands and suspension before resorting to dismissal. At one manufacturing firm, an employee's failure to call in when he or she will be absent from work may lead to a suspension after the third offense in a year. Suspension sends the employees a strong message that undesirable job behaviors must change, or termination is likely to follow.

Discharge: The Final Disciplinary Step

The final stage in the disciplinary process is termination. Both the positive and the progressive approaches to discipline clearly provide employees with warnings about the seriousness of their performance problems before dismissal occurs. Terminating workers because they do not keep their own promises is more likely to appear equitable and defensible to a jury.

FIGURE 9.4   Progressive Discipline Process

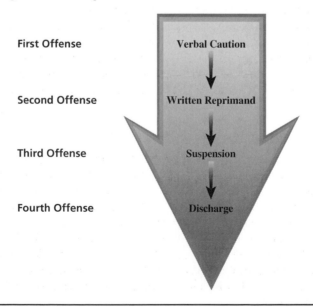

First Offense — Verbal Caution

Second Offense — Written Reprimand

Third Offense — Suspension

Fourth Offense — Discharge

NOTES

1. "Work Injuries and Illnesses," *Monthly Labor Review,* January 2004, 1.
2. "OSHA Inspections Increased in Fiscal '03," *Industrial Safety and Hygiene News,* January 2004, 8–9.
3. *Marshall v. Barlow's Inc.,* 98 S.Ct.1816(1978).
4. Marlene Piturro, "Workplace Violence," *Strategic Finance,* May 2001, 35–38.
5. Joan T. A. Gabel and Nancy R. Mansfield, "The Information Revolution and Its Impact on the Employment Relationship," *American Business Law Journal,* 40 (2003), 301–353.
6. Kirsten Martin and R. Edward Freeman, "Some Problems with Employee Monitoring," *Journal of Business Ethics,* April 2003, 353.
7. Gregory M. Davis, "Just the FACT Act, Please," *HR Magazine,* April 2004, 131–138.

INTERNET RESOURCES

Human Resources Law Index This Web site on workplace legal information discusses such issues as employment contracts and other issues. **http://www.hrlawindex.com**

Occupational Safety and Health Administration This Web site is the OSHA home page. Access to OSHA regulations for compliance, newsroom, and much more can be found here. **http://www.osha.gov**

SUGGESTED READINGS

Beyond Worker's Comp, National Safety Council, 2004.

Mark A. DeBernardo and Gina M. Pedro, *Guide to State and Federal Drug-Testing Laws,* Institute for a Drug-Free Workplace, 2005.

John H. McConnell, *How to Develop Essential HR Policies and Procedures,* AMACOM, 2004.

Lisa A. Milam-Perez, *Workplace Safety,* CCH, 2003.

Chapter 10

Labor Relations

A **union** is a formal association of workers that promotes the interests of its members through collective action. The state and nature of union/management relations vary among countries. In the United States, a complex system of laws, regulations, court decisions, and administrative rulings have clearly stated that workers may join unions when they wish to do so. Although fewer workers choose to do so today than before, the mechanisms remain for a union resurgence if employees feel that they need formal representation to deal with management.

Managerial Perspectives on HR

1. Agree or disagree with the following statement: "If management gets a union, it deserves one."

2. Why has union membership declined in the United States except in governmental sectors?

3. The HR manager, has heard rumors about potential efforts to unionize warehouse employees. What should be done?

NATURE OF UNIONS

Employers usually would rather not have to deal with unions because unions constrain what managers can and cannot do in a number of areas. Generally, union workers receive higher wages and benefits than do nonunion workers. In turn, unions *can* be associated with higher productivity, although management must find labor-saving ways of doing work to offset the higher labor costs.[1]

Some employers pursue a strategy of good relations with unions. Others may choose an aggressive, adversarial approach. Regardless of the type of employer, several common factors explain why employees unionize.

Why Employees Unionize

As Figure 10.1 shows, the major factors that can trigger unionization are issues of compensation, working environment, management style, and employee treatment. Whether a union targets a group of employees or the employees request union assistance, the union must win support from the employees to become their legal representative. Research over the years has consistently shown that employees join unions for two primary reasons: (1) they are dissatisfied with how they are treated

FIGURE 10.1 Factors Leading to Employee Unionization

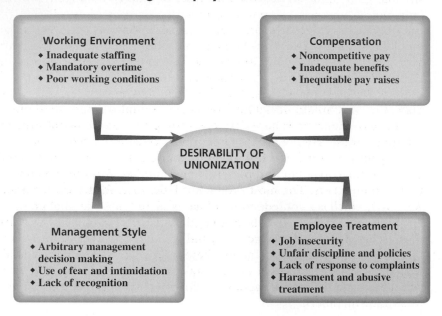

by their employers and (2) they believe that unions can improve their work situations. If employees do not receive what they perceive as fair from their employers, they may turn to unions for help obtaining what they believe is equitable.

The primary determinant of whether employees unionize is management. Reasonably competitive compensation, a good working environment, effective management and supervision, and fair and responsive treatment of workers all act as antidotes to unionization efforts. Unionization results when employees feel disrespected, unsafe, underpaid, and unappreciated, and see a union as a viable option. Once unionization occurs, the union's ability to foster commitment from members and to remain as their bargaining agent depends on how well the union succeeds in providing services that its members want. To prevent unionization, as well as to work effectively with unions already representing employees, both HR professionals and operating managers must be attentive and responsive to employees.

Global Labor Union Issues

In some countries, unions either do not exist at all or are relatively weak. Such is the case in China and a number of African countries. In other countries, unions are extremely strong and are closely tied to political parties.[2] Union membership is falling in many advanced countries, but collective bargaining is set in law as the way wages are determined in Europe. Some countries require that firms have union or worker representatives on their Boards of Directors. This practice, called **co-determination,** is common in European countries.

American labor is represented by many kinds of unions. But regardless of size and geographic scope, two basic types of unions developed over time. In a **craft union,** members do one type of work, often using specialized skills and training. Examples are the International Association of Bridge, Structural, Ornamental and Reinforcing Iron Workers, and the American Federation of Television and Radio Artists. An **industrial union** includes many persons working in the same industry or company, regardless of jobs held. The United Food and Commercial Workers, the United Auto Workers, and the American Federation of State, County, and Municipal Employees are examples of industrial unions.

Labor organizations have developed complex organizational structures with multiple levels. The broadest level is the **federation,** which is a group of autonomous national and international unions. A federation allows individual unions to work together and present a more unified front to the public, legislators, and members. The most prominent federation in the United States is the AFL-CIO, which is a confederation of national and international unions.

Like companies, unions find strength in size. In the past several years, about 40 mergers of unions have occurred, and a number of other unions have considered merging. For smaller unions, these mergers provide financial and union-organizing resources. Larger unions can add new members to cover managerial and administrative costs without spending funds to organize nonunion workers to become members.

UNION MEMBERSHIP IN THE UNITED STATES

The statistics on union membership tell a disheartening story for organized labor in the United States over the past several decades. Unions represented over 30% of the workforce from 1945 to 1960. But by 2004, unions in the United States represented less than 14% of all civilian workers and only 9.5% of the private-sector workforce. Even more disheartening for the unions, the actual number of members has declined in most years even though more people are employed than previously. Of the approximately 120 million U.S. workers, only about 16 million belong to a union.[3]

But within those averages, some unions have prospered. In the past several years, a few unions have organized thousands of janitors, health-care workers, cleaners, and other low-paid workers using publicity, pickets, boycotts, and strikes.

Public-Sector Unionism

Unions have had some measure of success with public-sector employees, particularly with state and local government workers. The government sector (federal, state, and local) is the most highly unionized part of the U.S. workforce.

Unionization of state and local government employees presents some unique problems and challenges. Allowing police officers, firefighters, and sanitation workers to strike endangers public health and safety. Consequently, more than 30 states have laws prohibiting work stoppages by public employees. These laws also identify a variety of ways to resolve negotiation impasses, including arbitration.

But unions still give employees in these areas greater security and better ability to influence decisions on wages and benefits.

Reasons for U.S. Union Membership Decline

Several issues have contributed to the decline of unions: deregulation, foreign competition, a larger number of people looking for jobs, and a general perception by firms that dealing with unions is expensive compared with nonunion alternatives. Also, management at many employers has taken a much more activist stance against unions than during the previous years of union growth. Also, unions are not as necessary for many workers, even though those workers enjoy the results of past union efforts to influence legislation.

Geographic Changes   Over the past decade, job growth in the United States has been the greatest in states located in the South, the Southwest, and the Rocky Mountains. Most of these states have "employer-friendly" laws, little tradition of unions, and relatively small percentages of unionized workers. Another issue involves the movement of many low-skill jobs outside the United States.

Workforce Changes   Many of the workforce and economic changes discussed in Chapter 1 have contributed to the decline in union representation of the labor force. The primary growth in jobs in the U.S. economy has been in technology, financial, and other service industries. There are growing numbers of white-collar employees including clerical workers, insurance claims representatives, data input processors, nurses, teachers, mental health aides, computer technicians, loan officers, auditors, and retail sales workers. Unions have increased efforts to organize white-collar workers as advances in technology have boosted their numbers in the workforce. However, unions face a major difficulty in organizing these workers. Many white-collar workers see unions as resistant to change and not in touch with the concerns of the more educated workers in technical and professional jobs. In addition, many white-collar workers exhibit a mentality and set of preferences quite different from those held by blue-collar union members.

The growing percentage of women in the U.S. workforce presents one challenge to unions. In the past, unions have not been as successful in organizing women workers as they have been in organizing men workers.

Another cause for the decline of unions is the shift in U.S. jobs from industries such as manufacturing, construction, and mining to service industries, as Figure 10.2 shows. There is a small percentage of union members in the financial services and wholesale/retail industries, the sectors in which many new jobs have been added, whereas the number of industrial jobs continues to shrink. In summary, union membership is primarily concentrated in the shrinking part of the economy, and unions are not making inroads into the fastest-growing segments in the U.S. economy.

To attempt to counteract the overall decline in union membership, unions are focusing on a number of industries and types of workers. Some frequently targeted groups are professionals, contingent and part-time workers, and low-skill workers.

FIGURE 10.2   Union Membership by Industry

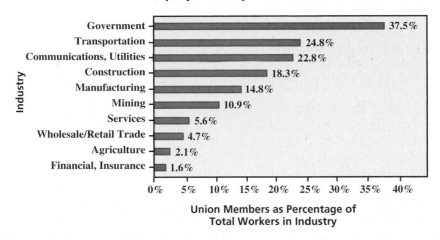

Union Members as Percentage of
Total Workers in Industry

BASIC LABOR LAW: "NATIONAL LABOR CODE"

The economic crises of the early 1930s and the restrictions on workers' ability to organize into unions led to the passage of landmark labor legislation. Later acts reflected other pressures and issues that required legislative attention.

Three acts, passed over a period of almost 25 years, constitute what has been labeled the "National Labor Code": (1) the Wagner Act, (2) the Taft-Hartley Act, and (3) the Landrum-Griffin Act. Each act was passed to focus on some facet of the relations between unions and management. Two other pieces of legislation, the Civil Service Reform Act and the Postal Reorganization Act, also affect various aspects of union/management relations.

Wagner Act (National Labor Relations Act)

The National Labor Relations Act, more commonly referred to as the Wagner Act, has been called the Magna Carta of labor and was, by anyone's standards, pro-union. Passed in 1935, the Wagner Act was an outgrowth of the Great Depression. With employers having to close or cut back their operations, workers were left with little job security. Unions stepped in to provide a feeling of solidarity and strength for many workers. The Wagner Act declared, in effect, that the official policy of the U.S. government was to encourage collective bargaining. Specifically, it established the right of workers to organize unhampered by management interference.

To protect union rights, the Wagner Act prohibited employers from utilizing unfair labor practices. Five of those practices are identified as follows:

▶ Interfering with, restraining, or coercing employees in the exercise of their right to organize or to bargain collectively

- ▶ Dominating or interfering with the formation or administration of any labor organization
- ▶ Encouraging or discouraging membership in any labor organization by discriminating with regard to hiring, tenure, or conditions of employment
- ▶ Discharging or otherwise discriminating against an employee because he or she filed charges or gave testimony under the act
- ▶ Refusing to bargain collectively with representatives of the employees

National Labor Relations Board (NLRB) The Wagner Act established the National Labor Relations Board as an independent entity to enforce the provisions of the act. The NLRB administers all provisions of the Wagner Act and of subsequent labor relations acts. The primary functions of the NLRB include conducting unionization elections, investigating complaints by employers or unions through its fact-finding process, issuing opinions on its findings, and prosecuting violations in court. The five members of the NLRB are appointed by the President of the United States and confirmed by the U.S. Senate.

Taft-Hartley Act (Labor-Management Relations Act)

The passage in 1947 of the Labor-Management Relations Act, better known as the Taft-Hartley Act, addressed the concerns of many who felt that unions had become too strong. The Taft-Hartley Act forbade unions from engaging in a series of unfair labor practices. Coercion, discrimination against nonmembers, refusing to bargain, excessive membership fees, and other practices were not allowed by unions.

National Emergency Strikes The Taft-Hartley Act allows the President of the United States to declare that a strike presents a national emergency. A **national emergency strike** is one that would impact an industry or a major part of it in such a way that the national economy would be significantly affected.

Right-to-Work Provision One specific provision of the Taft-Hartley Act, Section 14(b), deserves special explanation. This section allows states to pass laws that restrict compulsory union membership. Accordingly, some states have passed **right-to-work laws,** which prohibit requiring employees to join unions as a condition of obtaining or continuing employment. The laws were so named because they allow a person the right to work without having to join a union.

In states with right-to-work laws, employers may have an **open shop,** which indicates workers cannot be required to join or pay dues to a union. In states that do not have right-to-work laws, the following types of arrangements exist:

- ▶ *Union shop:* Requires that individuals join the union, usually 30–60 days after being hired.
- ▶ *Agency shop:* Requires employees who refuse to join the union to pay amounts equal to union dues and fees in return for the representation services of the union.

▶ *Maintenance-of-membership shop:* Requires workers to remain members of the union for the period of the labor contract.

Landrum-Griffin Act (Labor-Management Reporting and Disclosure Act)

The third segment of the National Labor Code, the Landrum-Griffin Act, was passed in 1959. Because a union is supposed to be a democratic institution in which union members vote on and elect officers and approve labor contracts, the Landrum-Griffin Act was passed in part to ensure that the federal government protects the democratic rights of those members. Under the Landrum-Griffin Act, unions are required to establish bylaws, make financial reports, and provide union members with a bill of rights. The law appointed the Secretary of Labor to act as a watchdog of union conduct.

Civil Service Reform Act of 1978

Passed as part of the Civil Service Reform Act of 1978, the Federal Service Labor-Management Relations statute made major changes in how the federal government deals with unions. The act also identified areas subject to bargaining and established the Federal Labor Relations Authority (FLRA) as an independent agency similar to the NLRB. The FLRA, a three-member body, was given the authority to oversee and administer union/management relations in the federal government and to investigate unfair practices in union-organizing efforts.

UNIONIZATION PROCESS

The typical union-organizing process is outlined in Figure 10.3. The process of unionizing an employer may begin in one of two primary ways: (1) a union targeting an industry or a company, or (2) employees requesting union representation. In the first case, the local or national union identifies a firm or an industry in which it believes unionization can succeed. In the second case, the impetus for union organizing occurs when individual workers in an organization contact a union and express a desire to unionize. The employees themselves—or the union—may then begin to campaign to win support among the other employees.

Employers may make strategic decisions and take aggressive steps to remain nonunion. Such a choice is perfectly rational, but may require some specific HR policies and philosophies. For example, "preventive" employee relations may emphasize good morale and loyalty based on concern for employees, competitive wages and benefits, a fair system for dealing with employee complaints, and safe working conditions. Other issues may also play a part in employees' decisions to stay nonunion, but if employers adequately address the points just listed, fewer workers are likely to feel the need for a union to represent them.

Once unionizing efforts begin, all activities must conform to the requirements established by applicable labor laws. Both management and the union

FIGURE 10.3 Typical Unionization Process

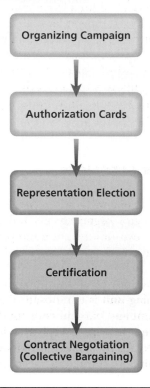

must adhere to those requirements, or the results of the effort can be appealed to the NLRB and overturned.

Organizing Campaign

Like other entities seeking members, a union usually mounts an organized campaign to persuade individuals to support its efforts. The persuasion takes many forms, including personally contacting employees outside work, mailing materials to employees' homes, inviting employees to attend special meetings away from the company, and publicizing the advantages of union membership. Many employers have a written "no-solicitation" policy to restrict employees and outsiders from distributing literature or soliciting union membership on company premises. Employers without such a policy may be unable to prevent those acts.

Unions sometimes pay organizers to infiltrate a targeted employer and try to organize workers. In this practice, known as **salting,** the unions hire and pay people to apply for jobs at certain companies; when the people are hired, they begin organizing efforts. The U.S. Supreme Court has ruled that refusing to hire otherwise qualified applicants, even if they are also paid by a union, violates the Wagner Act. However, employers may refuse to hire "salts" for job-related and nondiscriminatory reasons.

Authorization Cards

A **union authorization card** is signed by an employee to designate a union as her or his collective bargaining agent. At least 30% of the employees in the targeted group must sign authorization cards before an election can be called.

In reality, the fact that an employee signs an authorization card does not mean that the employee is in favor of a union; it means only that the employee would like the opportunity to vote on having a union. Employees who do not want a union might sign authorization cards because they want management to know they are disgruntled.

REPRESENTATION ELECTION

An election to determine if a union will represent the employees is supervised by the NLRB for private-sector organizations and by other legal bodies for public-sector organizations. If two unions are attempting to represent employees, the employees will have three choices: union A, union B, and no union.

Bargaining Unit Before any election, the appropriate bargaining unit must be determined. A **bargaining unit** is composed of all employees eligible to select a single union to represent and bargain collectively for them. If management and the union do not agree on who is and who is not included in the unit, the regional office of the NLRB must make the determination. Employees who constitute a bargaining unit have mutual interests in the following areas:

▶ Wages, hours, and working conditions
▶ Traditional industry groupings for bargaining purposes
▶ Physical location and amount of interaction and working relationships between employee groups
▶ Supervision by similar levels of management

Unfair Labor Practices Employers and unions engage in a number of activities before an election. Both the Wagner Act and the Taft-Hartley Act place restrictions on these activities.

Management representatives may use various tactics to defeat a unionization effort. Such tactics often begin when union publicity appears or during the distribution of authorization cards. Some employers hire experts who specialize in combating unionization efforts. Using these "union busters," as they are called by unions, appears to enhance employers' chances of winning the representation election. For example, Wal-Mart is one company that works hard to avoid unionization.

Election Process If an election is held, the union need receive only a *majority of the votes*. For example, if a group of 200 employees is the identified bargaining unit, and only 50 people vote, only 26 (50% of those voting plus 1) need to vote yes for the union to be named as the representative of all 200 employees.

Typically, the smaller the number of employees in the bargaining unit, the higher the likelihood that the union will win. If either side believes that the other side used unfair labor practices, the election results can be appealed to the NLRB.

Certification and Decertification

Official certification of a union as the legal representative for designated private-sector employees is given by the NLRB, or for public-sector employees by an equivalent body. Once certified, the union attempts to negotiate a contract with the employer. The employer *must* bargain; refusing to bargain with a certified union constitutes an unfair labor practice.

When members no longer wish to be represented by the union, they can use the election process to sever the relationship between themselves and the union. Similar to the unionization process, **decertification** is a process whereby a union is removed as the representative of a group of employees. Employees attempting to oust a union must obtain decertification authorization cards signed by at least 30% of the employees in the bargaining unit before an election may be called. If a majority of those voting in the election want to remove the union, the decertification effort succeeds. Current regulations prohibit employers from initiating or supporting decertification because it is a matter between employees and unions, and employers must stay out of the process.

Contract Negotiation (Collective Bargaining)

Collective bargaining, the last step in unionization, is the process whereby representatives of management and workers negotiate over wages, hours, and other terms and conditions of employment. This give-and-take process between representatives of the two organizations attempts to establish conditions beneficial to both. It is also a relationship based on relative power.

The power relationship in collective bargaining involves conflict, and the threat of conflict seems necessary to maintain the relationship. But perhaps the most significant aspect of collective bargaining is that it is a continuing relationship that does not end immediately after agreement is reached. Instead, it continues for the life of the labor agreement and beyond. Therefore, the more cooperative management is, the less hostility and conflict with unionized employees carries over to the workplace. However, this cooperation does not mean that the employer should give in to all union demands.

COLLECTIVE BARGAINING

A number of issues can be addressed during collective bargaining. Although not often listed as such in the contract, management rights and union security are two important issues subject to collective bargaining. These and other issues may be classified in several ways as discussed next. Virtually all labor contracts include **management rights,** which are rights reserved so that the employer can manage, direct, and control its business. By including such a provision, management attempts to preserve its unilateral right to make changes in areas not identified in a labor contract.

A major concern of union representatives when bargaining is the negotiation of **union security provisions,** which are contract clauses to help the union obtain and retain members. One union security provision is the *dues checkoff,* which provides for the automatic deduction of union dues from the payroll checks of union members. The dues checkoff makes it much easier for the union to collect its funds; without it, the union must collect dues by billing each member separately.

A growing type of union security in labor contracts is the *no-layoff policy,* or *job security guarantee.* Such a provision is especially important to many union workers because of all the mergers, downsizings, and job reductions taking place in many industries.

The NLRB has defined collective bargaining issues in three ways. Issues identified specifically by labor laws or court decisions as subject to bargaining are *mandatory issues.* If either party demands that issues in this category be subject to bargaining, then that must occur. Generally, mandatory issues relate to wages, benefits, nature of jobs, and other work-related subjects. Issues that are not mandatory and that relate to certain jobs are *permissive issues.* For example, the following issues can be bargained over if both parties agree: benefits for retired employees, product prices for employees, or performance bonds.

A final category, *illegal issues,* includes those issues that would require either party to take illegal action. Examples would be giving preference to union members when hiring employees or demanding a closed shop provision in the contract. If one side wants to bargain over an illegal issue, the other side can refuse.

COLLECTIVE BARGAINING PROCESS

The collective bargaining process consists of a number of stages: preparation and initial demands, negotiations, settlement or impasse, and strikes and lockouts. Throughout the process, management and labor deal with the terms of their relationship.

Preparation and Initial Demands

Both labor and management representatives spend much time preparing for negotiations. Employer and industry data concerning wages, benefits, working conditions, management and union rights, productivity, and absenteeism are gathered. If the organization argues that it cannot afford to pay what the union is asking, the employer's financial situation and accompanying data become all the more relevant. However, the union must request such information before the employer is obligated to provide it. Typical bargaining includes initial proposals of expectations by both sides.

Continuing Negotiations

After taking initial positions, each side attempts to determine what the other side values highly so that the best bargain can be struck. For example, the union may be asking the employer to pay for dental benefits as part of a package that also includes wage increases and retirement benefits. However, the union may be most interested in the retirement benefits, and may be willing to trade the dental payments for better retirement benefits. Management must determine what the union has as a priority and decide exactly what to give up. It is common for wages and benefits to be higher in unionized firms.[4]

Provisions in federal law require that both employers and union bargaining representatives negotiate in good faith. In good-faith negotiations, the parties agree to send negotiators who can bargain and make decisions, rather than people who do not have the authority to commit either group to a decision. Meetings between the parties cannot be scheduled at absurdly inconvenient hours. Some give-and-take discussions also must occur.

Settlement and Contract Agreement

After reaching an initial agreement, the bargaining parties usually return to their respective constituencies to determine if the informal agreement is acceptable. A particularly crucial stage is **ratification** of the labor agreement, which occurs when union members vote to accept the terms of a negotiated agreement. Before ratification, the union negotiating team explains the agreement to the union members and presents it for a vote. If the members approve the agreement, it is then formalized into a contract.

Bargaining Impasse

Regardless of the structure of the bargaining process, labor and management do not always reach agreement on the issues. If they reach an impasse, then the disputes can be taken to conciliation, mediation, or arbitration.

Conciliation and Mediation When an impasse occurs, an outside party such as the Federal Mediation and Conciliation Service may help the two deadlocked parties to continue negotiations and arrive at a solution. In **conciliation,** the third party attempts to keep union and management negotiators talking so that they can reach a voluntary settlement, but makes no proposals for solutions. In **mediation,** the third party helps the negotiators to reach a settlement. In neither conciliation nor mediation does the third party attempt to impose a solution. Sometimes, *fact-finding* helps to clarify the issues of disagreement as an intermediate step between mediation and arbitration.

Arbitration In **arbitration,** a neutral third party makes a decision. Arbitration can be conducted by an individual or a panel of individuals. Fortunately, in many situations, agreements are reached through negotiations without the need for arbitration.[5] When disagreements continue, strikes or lockouts may occur.

Strikes and Lockouts

If a deadlock cannot be resolved, then an employer may revert to a lockout—or a union may revert to a strike. During a **strike,** union members refuse to work in order to put pressure on an employer. Often, the striking union members picket or demonstrate against the employer outside the place of business by carrying placards and signs. In a **lockout,** management shuts down company operations to prevent union members from working. This action may avert possible damage or sabotage to company facilities or injury to employees who continue to work.

Union/Management Cooperation

The adversarial relationship that naturally exists between unions and management may lead to strikes and lockouts. However, such conflicts are relatively rare. Even more encouraging is the growing recognition on the part of union leaders and employer representatives that cooperation between management and labor unions offers the most sensible route if organizations are to compete effectively in a global economy.[6]

Employee Involvement Programs

Suggesting that union/management cooperation or involving employees in making suggestions and decisions could be bad seems a little illogical. Yet, some decisions by the NLRB appear to have done just that. One key to decisions allowing employee involvement committees and programs seems to be that these entities not deal directly with traditional collective bargaining issues such as wages, hours, and working conditions. Other keys are that the committees be composed primarily of workers and that they have broad authority to make operational suggestions and decisions.

Unions and Employee Ownership

Unions in some situations have encouraged workers to become partial or complete owners of the companies that employ them. These efforts were spurred by concerns that firms were preparing to shut down, merge, or be bought out, resulting in a cut in the number of union jobs and workers.

GRIEVANCE MANAGEMENT

Unions know that employee dissatisfaction is a potential source of trouble for employers, whether it is expressed or not. Hidden dissatisfaction grows and creates reactions that may be completely out of proportion to the original concerns. Therefore, it is important that dissatisfaction be given an outlet. A **complaint,** which is merely an indication of employee dissatisfaction, is one outlet. Complaints often are made by employees who are not represented by unions.

If an employee is represented by a union, and the employee says, "I should have received the job transfer because I have more seniority, which is what the union contract states," and he or she submits it in writing, then that complaint becomes a grievance. A **grievance** is a complaint formally stated in writing.

Management should be concerned with both complaints and grievances, because both indicate potential problems within the workforce. Without a grievance procedure, management may be unable to respond to employee concerns because managers are unaware of them. Therefore, a formal grievance procedure provides a valuable communication tool for the organization, which also is beneficial for maintaining and improving employee relations.

Grievance Procedures

Grievance procedures are formal channels of communication designed to settle grievances as soon as possible after problems arise. First-line supervisors are usually closest to a problem. However, these supervisors are concerned with many other matters besides one employee's grievance, and may even be the subject of an employee's grievance. To receive the appropriate attention, grievances go through a specific process for resolution.

Steps in a Grievance Procedure

Grievance procedures can vary in the number of steps they include. Figure 10.4 shows a typical grievance procedure, which consists of the following steps:

1. The employee discusses the grievance with the union steward (the representative of the union on the job) and the supervisor.
2. The union steward discusses the grievance with the supervisor's manager and/or the HR manager.

FIGURE 10.4   Steps a Typical Grievance Procedure

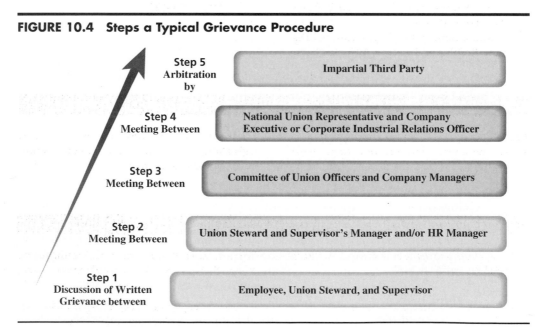

Step 5 Arbitration by	Impartial Third Party
Step 4 Meeting Between	National Union Representative and Company Executive or Corporate Industrial Relations Officer
Step 3 Meeting Between	Committee of Union Officers and Company Managers
Step 2 Meeting Between	Union Steward and Supervisor's Manager and/or HR Manager
Step 1 Discussion of Written Grievance between	Employee, Union Steward, and Supervisor

3. A committee of union officers discusses the grievance with appropriate company managers.
4. The representative of the national union discusses the grievance with designated company executives or the corporate industrial relations officer.
5. If the grievance is not solved at this stage, it goes to arbitration.[7] An impartial third party may ultimately dispose the grievance.

Grievance arbitration is a means by which a third party settles disputes arising from different interpretations of a labor contract. This process should not be confused with contract or issues arbitration, discussed earlier, in which arbitration is used to determine how a contract will be written. The U.S. Supreme Court has ruled that grievance arbitration decisions issued under labor contract provisions are enforceable. Grievance arbitration includes more than 50 topic areas, with discipline and discharge, safety and health, and security issues being most prevalent.

NOTES

1. Barry T. Hirsch, "What Do Unions Do for Economic Performance?" *Discussion Paper Series IZA DP No. 892,* Institute for the Study of Labor, October 2003.
2. International Labor Organization, *http://www.ilo.org.*
3. For details, see *http://www.bls.gov.*
4. Bruce E. Kaufman, "Models of Union Wage Determination," *Industrial Relations,* 41 (2002), 110–157.
5. Corinne Bendersky, "Organizational Dispute Resolution Systems: A Complementaries Model," *Academy of Management Review,* 28 (2003), 643–656.
6. Sarah Oxenbridge and William Brown, "The Two Faces of Partnership?" *Employee Relations,* 24 (2002), 262–276.
7. William M. Haraway III, "Rediscovering Process Values in Employee Grievance Procedures," *Administration and Society,* 34 (2002), 499–521.

INTERNET RESOURCES

AFL-CIO   The AFL-CIO's homepage provides union movement information. **http://www.aflcio.org**

Labornet   This site describes unions, news, legislation, and upcoming union events. **http://www.labornet.org**

SUGGESTED READINGS

T. O. Collier, *Supervisor's Guide to Labor Relations,* SHRM, 2001.

Court D. Gifford, *Directory of U.S. Labor Organizations,* Bureau of National Affairs, 2005.

William H. Holley, Kenneth M. Jennings, and Roger S. Wolters, *The Labor Relations Process,* 8th ed., Thomson Learning, 2005.

Charles S. Loughran, *Negotiating a Labor Contract,* Bureau of National Affairs, 2003.

Appendix A

Major Federal Equal Employment Opportunity Laws and Regulations

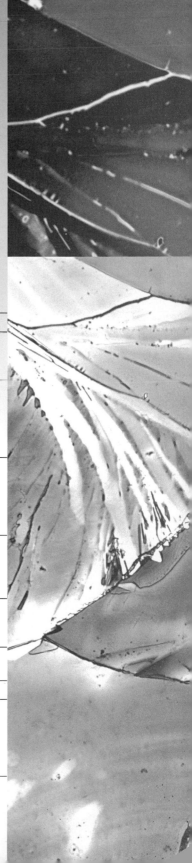

Act	Year	Key Provisions
Broad-Based Discrimination		
Title VII, Civil Rights Act of 1964	1964	Prohibits discrimination in employment on basis of race, color, religion, sex, or national origin
Executive Orders 11246 and 11375	1965 1967	Require federal contractors and subcontractors to eliminate employment discrimination and prior discrimination through affirmative action
Executive Order 11478	1969	Prohibits discrimination in the U.S. Postal Service and in the various government agencies on the basis of race, color, religion, sex, national origin, handicap, or age
Vietnam Era Veterans' Readjustment Assistance Act	1974	Prohibits discriminations against Vietnam-era veterans by federal contractors and the U.S. government and requires affirmative action
Civil Rights Act of 1991	1991	Overturns several past Supreme Court decisions and changes damage claims provisions
Congressional Accountability Act	1995	Extends EEO and Civil Rights Act provisions to U.S. congressional staff
Race/National Origin Discrimination		
Immigration Reform and Control Act	1986 1990 1996	Establishes penalties for employers who knowingly hire illegal aliens; prohibits employment discrimination on the basis of national origin or citizenship

Gender/Sex Discrimination

Equal Pay Act	1963	Requires equal pay for men and women performing substantially the same work
Pregnancy Discrimination Act	1978	Prohibits discrimination against women affected by pregnancy, childbirth, or related medical conditions; requires that they be treated as all other employees for employment-related purposes, including benefits

Age Discrimination

Age Discrimination in Employment Act (as amended in 1978 and 1986)	1967	Prohibits discrimination against persons over age 40 and restricts mandatory retirement requirements, except where age is a bona fide occupational qualification
Older Workers Benefit Protection Act of 1990	1990	Prohibits age-based discrimination in early retirement and other benefits plans

Disability Discrimination

Vocational Rehabilitation Act and Rehabilitation Act of 1974	1973 1974	Prohibit employers with federal contracts over $2,500 from discriminating against individuals with disabilities
Americans with Disabilities Act	1990	Requires employer accommodations for individuals with disabilities

Appendix B

Guidelines to Lawful and Unlawful Preemployment Inquiries

Subject of Inquiry	It May Not Be Discriminatory to Inquire About . . .	It May Be Discriminatory to Inquire About . . .
1. Name	a. Whether applicant has ever worked under a different name	a. The original name of applicant whose name has been legally changed b. The ethnic association of applicant's name
2. Age	a. If applicant is over the age of 18 b. If applicant is under the age of 18 or 21 if that information is job related (e.g., for selling liquor in a retail store)	a. Date of birth b. Date of high school graduation
3. Residence	a. Applicant's place of residence b. Alternative contact information	a. Previous addresses b. Birthplace of applicant or applicant's parents c. Length lived at current and previous addresses
4. Race or Color		a. Applicant's race or color of applicant's skin
5. National Origin and Ancestry		a. Applicant's lineage, ancestry, national origin, parentage, or nationality b. Nationality of applicant's parents or spouse
6. Sex and Family Composition		a. Sex of applicant b. Marital status of applicant c. Dependents of applicants or child-care arrangements d. Whom to contact in case of emergency
7. Creed or Religion		a. Applicant's religious affiliation b. Applicant's church, parish, mosque, or synagogue c. Holidays observed by applicant

Subject of Inquiry	It May Not Be Discriminatory to Inquire About . . .	It May Be Discriminatory to Inquire About . . .
8. Citizenship	a. Whether the applicant is a U.S. citizen or has a current permit/visa to work in the U.S.	a. Whether applicant is a citizen of a country other than the U.S. b. Date of citizenship
9. Language	a. Language applicant speaks and/or writes fluently, if job related	a. Applicant's native tongue b. Language used at home
10. References	a. Names of persons willing to provide professional and/or character references for applicant b. Previous work contacts	a. Name of applicant's religious leader b. Political affiliation and contacts
11. Relatives	a. Names of relatives already employed by the employer	a. Name and/or address of any relative of applicant b. Whom to contact in case of emergency
12. Organizations	a. Applicant's membership in any professional, service, or trade organization	a. All clubs or social organizations to which applicant belongs
13. Arrest Record and Convictions	a. Convictions, if related to job performance (disclaimer should accompany)	a. Number and kinds of arrests b. Convictions, unless related to job requirements and performance
14. Photographs		a. Photographs with application, with resume, or before hiring
15. Height and Weight		a. Any inquiry into height and weight of applicant, except where a BFOQ exists
16. Physical Limitations	a. Whether applicant has the ability to perform job-related functions with or without accommodation	a. The nature or severity of an illness or physical condition b. Whether applicant has ever filed a workers' compensation claim c. Any recent or past operations, treatments, or surgeries and dates
17. Education	a. Training applicant has received, if related to the job b. Highest level of education applicant has attained, if validated that having certain educational background (e.g., high school diploma or college degree) is needed to perform the specific job	a. Date of high school graduation
18. Military	a. Branch of the military applicant served in and ranks attained b. Type of education or training received in military	a. Military discharge details b. Military service records
19. Financial Status		a. Applicant's debts or assets b. Garnishments

Appendix C

Sample Job Description

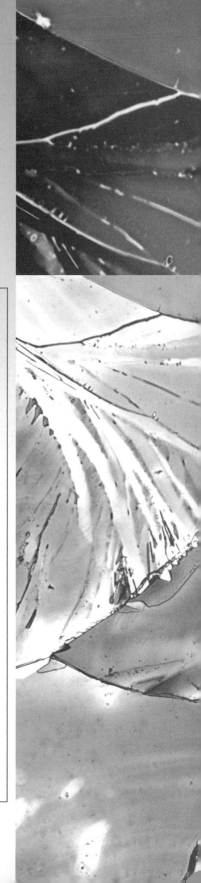

Identification Section:

Position Title: Human Resource Manager

Department: Human Resources

Reports to: President

EEOC Class: O/M

FLSA Status: Exempt

General Summary: Directs HR activities of the firm to ensure compliance with laws and policies, and assists President with overall HR planning

Essential Job Functions:

1. Manages compensation and benefits programs for all employees, resolves compensation and benefits questions from employees, and negotiates with benefits carriers (20%)
2. Ensures compliance with both internal policies and applicable state and federal regulations and laws, including EEO, OSHA, and FLSA (20%)
3. Identifies HR planning issues and suggested approaches to President and other senior managers (15%)
4. Assists managers and supervisors create, plan, and conduct training and various development programs for new and existing employees (15%)
5. Recruits candidates for employment over telephone and in person. Interviews and selects internal and external candidates for open positions (10%)
6. Reviews and updates job descriptions, assisted by department supervisors, and coordinates performance appraisal process to ensure timely reviews are completed for all employees (10%)
7. Administers various HR policies and procedures and helps managers resolve employee performance and policy issues (10%)
8. Performs other duties as needed and directed by President

Knowledge, Skills, and Abilities:

► Knowledge of HR policies, HR practices, and HR-related laws and regulations
► Knowledge of company products and services, and policies and procedures
► Knowledge of management principles and practices
► Skill in operating equipment, such as personal computer, software, and IT systems
► Skill in oral and written communication
► Ability to communicate with employees and various business contacts in a professional and courteous manner
► Ability to organize multiple work assignments and establish priorities
► Ability to negotiate with others and resolve conflicts, particularly in sensitive situations
► Ability to pay close attention to detail and to ensure accuracy of reports and data
► Ability to make sound decisions using available information while maintaining confidentiality
► Ability to create a team environment and sustain employee commitment

Education and Experience: Bachelor's degree in HR management or equivalent, plus 3–5 years' experience

Physical Requirements:	Percentage of Work Time Spent on Activity			
	0%–24%	25%–49%	50%–74%	75%–100%
Seeing: Must be able to read computer screen and various reports				X
Hearing: Must be able to hear well enough to communicate with employees and others				X
Standing/walking	X			
Climbing/stooping/kneeling	X			
Lifting/pulling/pushing	X			
Fingering/grasping/feeling: Must be able to write, type, and use phone system				X

Working Conditions: Good working conditions with the absence of disagreeable conditions.

Note: The statements herein are intended to describe the general nature and level of work performed by employees, but are not a complete list of responsibilities, duties, and skills required of personnel so classified. Furthermore, they do not establish a contract for employment and are subject to change at the discretion of the employer.

Appendix D

Effective Interviewing

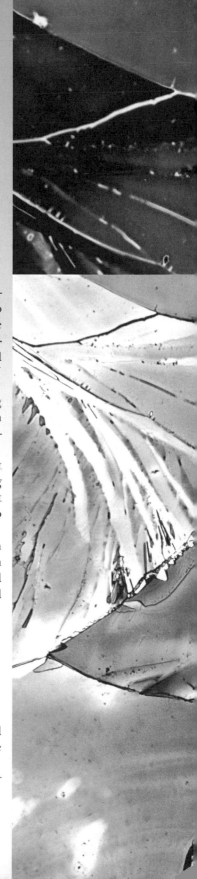

Many people think that the ability to interview is an innate talent, but this contention is difficult to support. Just being personable and liking to talk is no guarantee that someone will be an effective interviewer. Interviewing skills are developed through training. A number of suggestions for making interviewing more effective have been developed. Three key ones commonly cited are as follows:

- *Plan the interview:* Interviewers should review preemployment screening information, the application or resume, and the appropriate job description before beginning the interview, and then identify specific areas for questioning during the interview.
- *Control the interview:* This includes knowing in advance what information must be collected, systematically collecting it during the interview, and stopping when that information has been collected. Controlling the interview does not mean monopolizing the conversation; effective interviewers should talk no more than about 25% of the time in an in-depth interview.
- *Use effective questioning techniques:* The questioning techniques used by an interviewer can and do significantly affect the type and quality of information obtained. *Describe, who, what, when, why, tell me, how,* and *which* are all good words and phrases for beginning questions that will produce longer and more informative answers.

QUESTIONS TO AVOID

Certain kinds of questions should be avoided in selection interviews:

- *Yes/no questions:* Unless verifying specific information, the interviewer should avoid questions that can be answered "Yes" or "No." For example, "Did you have good attendance on your last job?" will probably be answered simply, "Yes."
- *Obvious questions:* An obvious question is one for which the interviewer already has the answer and the applicant knows it.

▶ *Questions that rarely produce a true answer:* An example is, "How did you get along with your coworkers?" The likely answer is, "Just fine."

▶ *Leading questions:* A leading question is one to which the answer is obvious from the way that the question is asked. For example, "How do you like working with other people?" suggests the answer, "I like it."

▶ *Illegal questions:* Questions that involve information such as race, age, gender, national origin, marital status, and number of children are illegal. They are just as inappropriate in the interview as on the application form.

▶ *Questions that are not job related:* All questions should be directly related to the job for which the interviewee has applied.

Appendix E

Legal Do's and Don'ts for Managers during the Unionization

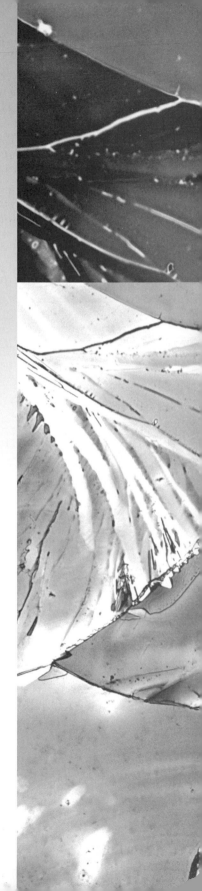

Do (legal)

- Tell employees about current wages and benefits and how they compare with those in other firms
- Tell employees that the employer opposes unionization
- Tell employees the disadvantages of having a union (especially cost of dues, assessments, and requirements of membership)
- Show employees articles about unions and relate negative experiences elsewhere
- Explain the unionization process to employees accurately
- Forbid distribution of union literature during work hours in work areas
- Enforce disciplinary policies and rules consistently and appropriately

Don't (illegal)

- Promise employees pay increases or promotions if they vote against the union
- Threaten employees with termination or discriminate when disciplining employees
- Threaten to close down or move the company if a union is voted on
- Spy on or have someone spy on union meetings
- Make a speech to employees or groups at work within 24 hours of the election (before that, it is allowed)
- Ask employees how they plan to vote or if they have signed authorization cards
- Encourage employees to persuade others to vote against the union (such persuasion must be initiated solely by employees)

Glossary

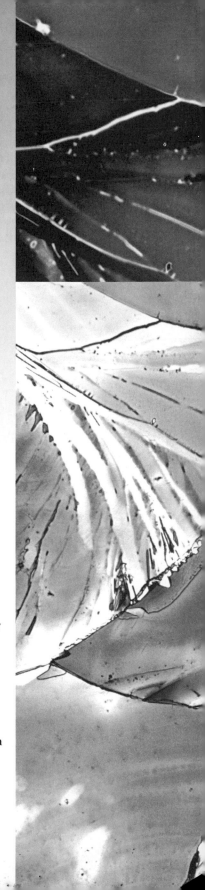

Acceptance rate Percent of applicants hired divided by total number of applicants.

Affirmative action Employers are urged to hire groups of people based on their race, age, gender, or national origin, to make up for historical discrimination.

Affirmative Action Plan (AAP) Formal document that an employer compiles annually for submission to enforcement agencies.

Arbitration Process that uses a neutral third party to make a decision.

Assessment centers Collections of instruments and exercises designed to diagnose individuals' development needs.

Availability analysis Identifies the number of protected-class members available to work in the appropriate labor markets for given jobs.

Bargaining unit Employees eligible to select a single union to represent and bargain collectively for them.

Base pay Basic compensation that an employee receives, usually as a wage or a salary.

Behavioral interview Interview in which applicants give specific examples of how they have performed a certain task or handled a problem in the past.

Behavior modeling Copying someone else's behavior.

Benchmarking Comparing specific measures of performance against data on the measures in other organizations.

Benchmark jobs Jobs found in many organizations.

Benefit Indirect reward given to an employee or a group of employees for organizational membership.

Bona fide occupational qualification (BFOQ) Characteristic providing a legitimate reason why an employer can exclude persons on otherwise illegal bases of consideration.

Bonus One-time payment that does not become part of the employee's base pay.

Burden of proof What individuals who file suit against employers must prove in order to establish that illegal discrimination has occurred.

Business necessity Practice necessary for safe and efficient organizational operations.

Career Series of work-related positions a person occupies throughout life.

Cash balance plan Retirement program in which benefits are based on an accumulation of annual company contributions, expressed as a percentage of pay, plus interest credited each year.

Central tendency error Occurs when a rater gives all employees a score within a narrow range in the middle of the scale.

Closed shop Firm that requires individuals to join a union before they can be hired.

Co-determination Practice whereby union or worker representatives are given positions on a company's Board of Directors.

Cognitive ability tests Tests that measure individual abilities such as thinking, memory, reasoning, verbal, and mathematical.

Collective bargaining Process whereby representatives of management and workers negotiate over wages, hours, and other terms and conditions of employment.

Commission Compensation computed as a percentage of sales in units or dollars.

Compa-ratio Pay level divided by the midpoint of the pay range.

Compensable factor Factor that identifies a job value commonly present throughout a group of jobs.

Compensation committee Subgroup of the Board of Directors, composed of directors who are not officers of the firm.

Compensatory time off Hours given to an employee in lieu of payment for extra time worked.

Competencies Individual capabilities that can be linked to enhanced performance by individuals or teams.

Competency-based pay Rewards individuals for the capabilities they demonstrate and acquire.

Complaint Indication of employee dissatisfaction.

Conciliation Process by which a third party attempts to keep union and management negotiators talking so that they can reach a voluntary settlement.

Constructive discharge Deliberately making conditions intolerable to get an employee to quit.

Consumer-driven health (CDH) plan One that provides employer financial contributions to employees to cover their own health-related expenses.

Content validity Validity measured by a logical, non-statistical method to identify the KSAs and other characteristics necessary to perform a job.

Contractual rights Rights based on a specific contract between an employer and an employee.

Contrast error Tendency to rate people relative to others rather than against performance standards.

Co-payment Strategy requiring employees to pay a portion of the cost of insurance premiums, medical care, and prescription drugs.

Core competency A unique capability that creates high value and differentiates an organization from its competition.

Cost-benefit analysis Comparison of costs and benefits associated with training.

Craft union One whose members do one type of work, often using specialized skills and training.

Criterion-related validity Validity measured by a procedure that uses a test as the predictor of how well an individual will perform on the job.

Cross training Training people to do more than one job.

Cumulative trauma disorders (CTDs) Muscle and skeletal injuries that occur when workers repetitively use the same muscles to perform tasks.

Decertification Process whereby a union is removed as the representative of a group of employees.

Defined-benefit plan Retirement program in which an employee is promised a pension amount based on age and service.

Defined-contribution plan Retirement program in which the employer makes an annual payment to an employee's pension account.

Development Efforts to improve employees' abilities to handle a variety of assignments and to cultivate employees' capabilities beyond those required by the current job.

Disabled person Someone who has a physical or mental impairment that substantially limits his life activities, who has a record of such impairment, or who is regarded as having such an impairment.

Discipline Form of training that enforces organizational rules.

Disparate impact Occurs when members of a protected class are substantially underrepresented as a result of employment decisions that work to their disadvantage.

Disparate treatment Occurs when members of a protected class are treated differently from others.

Distributive justice Perceived fairness in the distribution of outcomes.

Dual-career ladder System that allows a person to advance up either a management ladder or a corresponding ladder on the technical/professional side of a career.

Duty Larger work segment composed of several tasks that are performed by an individual.

Economic value added (EVA) Net operating profit of a firm after the cost of capital is deducted.

E-learning Use of the Internet or an organizational intranet to conduct training online.

Employee stock ownership plan (ESOP) Plan whereby employees have significant stock ownership in their employers.

Employment-at-will (EAW) Common-law doctrine stating that employers have the right to hire, fire, demote, or promote whomever they choose, unless there is a law or a contract to the contrary.

Employment contract Agreement that formally outlines the details of employment.

Entitlement philosophy Assumes that individuals who have worked another year are entitled to pay increases, with little regard for performance differences.

Equal employment Employment that is not affected by illegal discrimination.

Equity Perceived fairness between what a person does and what the person receives.

Ergonomics Study and design of the work environment to address physiological and physical demands on individuals.

Essential job functions Fundamental duties of a job.

Exempt employees Employees to whom employers are not required to pay overtime under the Fair Labor Standards Act.

Exit interview An interview in which individuals are asked to give their reasons for leaving the organization.

Federation Group of autonomous national and international unions.

Flexible benefits plan Program that allows employees to select the benefits they prefer from groups of benefits established by the employer.

Flexible staffing Use of workers who are not traditional employees.

Flextime Scheduling arrangement in which employees work a set number of hours a day but vary starting and ending times.

Forced distribution Performance appraisal method in which ratings of employees' performance are distributed along a bell-shaped curve.

Forecasting Using information from the past and the present to identify expected future conditions.

4/5ths rule Discrimination exists if the selection rate for a protected group is less than 80% (4/5ths) of the selection rate for the majority group or less than 80% of the majority group's representation in the relevant labor market.

Gainsharing System of sharing with employees greater-than-expected gains in profits and/or productivity.

Garnishment A court action in which a portion of an employee's wages is set aside to pay a debt owed a creditor.

Glass ceiling Discriminatory practices that have prevented women and other protected-class members from advancing to executive-level jobs.

Graphic rating scale Scale that allows the rater to mark an employee's performance on a continuum.

Grievance Complaint formally stated in writing.

Grievance arbitration Means by which a third party settles disputes arising from different interpretations of a labor contract.

Grievance procedures Formal channels of communication used to resolve grievances.

Halo effect Occurs when a rater scores an employee high on all job criteria because of performance in one area.

Health General state of physical, mental, and emotional well-being.

Health maintenance organization (HMO) Plan that provides services for a fixed period on a prepaid basis.

Health promotion Supportive approach of facilitating and encouraging healthy actions and lifestyles among employees.

Hostile environment Sexual harassment in which an individual's work performance or psychological well-being is unreasonably affected by intimidating or offensive working conditions.

HR audit Formal research effort that evaluates the current state of HR management in an organization.

HR generalist A person who has responsibility for performing a variety of HR activities.

HR metrics Specific measures tied to HR performance indicators.

HR specialist A person who has in-depth knowledge and expertise in a limited area of HR.

Human capital The collective value of the capabilities, knowledge, skills, life experiences, and motivation of an organizational workforce.

Human resource (HR) management The direction of organizational systems to ensure that human talent is used effectively and efficiently to accomplish organizational goals.

Human resource (HR) planning Process of analyzing and identifying the need for and availability of human resources so that the organization can meet its objectives.

Human resource management system (HRMS) An integrated system providing information used by HR management in decision making.

Illegal issues Collective bargaining issues that would require either party to take illegal action.

Immediate confirmation Based on the idea that people learn best if reinforcement and feedback are given after training.

Individual-centered career planning Career planning focusing on an individual's career rather than on organizational needs.

Industrial union One that includes many persons working in the same industry or company, regardless of jobs held.

Informal training Training that occurs through interactions and feedback among employees.

Job analysis A systematic way of gathering and analyzing information about what people are doing in various jobs, and what skills are needed to do them.

Job criteria Important elements in a given job.

Job description Identification of the tasks, duties, and responsibilities of a job.

Job design Organizing tasks, duties, and responsibilities into a productive unit of work.

Job evaluation Formal, systematic means to identify the relative worth of jobs within an organization.

Job family Group of jobs having common organizational characteristics.

Job posting System in which the employer provides notices of job openings and employees respond by applying.

Job satisfaction A positive emotional state resulting from evaluating one's job experiences.

Job sharing Scheduling arrangement in which two employees perform the work of one full-time job.

Job specifications The knowledge, skills, and abilities (KSAs) an individual needs to perform a job satisfactorily.

Knowledge management The way an organization identifies and leverages knowledge in order to be competitive.

Labor markets External supply pool from which organizations attract employees.

Leniency error Occurs when ratings of all employees fall at the high end of the scale.

Living wage One that is supposed to meet the basic needs of a worker's family.

Lockout Shutdown of company operations undertaken by management to prevent union members from working.

Lump-sum increase (LSI) One-time payment of all or part of a yearly pay increase.

Managed care Approaches that monitor and reduce medical costs through restrictions and market system alternatives.

Management by objectives (MBO) Performance appraisal method that specifies the performance goals that an individual and manager mutually identify.

Management rights Rights reserved so that the employer can manage, direct, and control its business.

Mandatory issues Collective bargaining issues identified specifically by labor laws or court decisions as subject to bargaining.

Marginal job functions Duties that are part of a job but are incidental or ancillary to the purpose and nature of the job.

Market pricing Use of pay survey data to identify the relative value of jobs based on what other employers pay for similar jobs.

Mediation Process by which a third party helps the negotiators to reach a settlement.

Motivation The desire within a person causing that person to act.

National emergency strike Strike that would impact the national economy significantly.

Nonexempt employees Employees who must be paid overtime under the Fair Labor Standards Act.

Open shop Workers are not required to join or pay dues to a union.

Organizational commitment The degree to which employees believe in and accept organizational goals and desire to remain with the organization.

Organizational culture The shared values and beliefs in an organization.

Organization-centered career planning Career planning that focuses on identifying career paths that provide for the logical progression of people between jobs in an organization.

Orientation Planned introduction of new employees to their jobs, coworkers, and the organization.

Paid-time-off (PTO) plans Plans that combine all sick leaves, vacation time, and holidays into a total number of hours or days that employees can take off with pay.

Panel interview Interview in which several interviewers meet with the candidate at the same time.

Pay compression Occurs when the pay differences among individuals with different levels of experience and performance become small.

Pay equity Similarity in pay for all jobs requiring comparable knowledge, skills, and abilities, even if actual duties and market rates differ significantly.

Pay-for-performance philosophy Requires that compensation changes reflect individual performance differences.

Pay grades Groupings of individual jobs having approximately the same job worth.

Pay survey Collection of data on compensation rates for workers performing similar jobs in other organizations.

Pension plan Retirement program established and funded by the employer and employees.

Performance appraisal Process of evaluating how well employees perform their jobs and then communicating that information to the employees.

Performance consulting Process in which a trainer and the organizational client work together to determine what needs to be done to improve results.

Performance management Composed of the processes used to identify, measure, communicate, develop, and reward employee performance.

Performance standards Indicators of what the job accomplishes and how performance is measured in key areas of the job description.

Permissive issues Collective bargaining issues that are not mandatory and relate to certain jobs.

Perquisites (perks) Special benefits—usually non-cash items—for executives.

Person/job fit Matching the KSAs of people with the characteristics of jobs.

Physical ability tests Tests that measure an individual's abilities such as strength, endurance, and muscular movement.

Placement Fitting a person to the right job.

Policies General guidelines that focus organizational actions.

Predictors Measurable or visible indicators of a selection criterion.

Preferred provider organization (PPO) A health-care provider that contracts with an employer group to supply health-care services to employees at a competitive rate.

Primacy effect Occurs when a rater gives greater weight to information received first when appraising an individual's performance.

Procedural justice Perceived fairness of the process and procedures used to make decisions about employees.

Procedures Customary methods of handling activities.

Profit sharing System to distribute a portion of the profits of the organization of employees.

Protected class Individuals within a group identified for protection under equal employment laws and regulations.

Psychological contract The unwritten expectations employees and employers have about the nature of their work relationships.

Quid pro quo Sexual harassment in which employment outcomes are linked to the individual granting sexual favors.

Ranking Performance appraisal method in which all employees are listed from highest to lowest in performance.

Rater bias Occurs when a rater's values or prejudices distort the rating.

Ratification Process by which union members vote to accept the terms of a negotiated labor agreement.

Realistic job preview (RJP) Process through which a job applicant receives an accurate picture of a job.

Reasonable accommodation A modification or adjustment to a job or work environment for a qualified individual with a disability.

Recency effect Occurs when a rater gives greater weight to information received first when appraising an individual's performance.

Recruiting Process of generating a pool of qualified applicants for organizational jobs.

Reinforcement Based on the idea that people tend to repeat responses that give them some type of positive reward and avoid actions associated with negative consequences.

Repatriation Planning, training, and reassignment of global employees to their home countries.

Responsibilities Obligations to perform certain tasks and duties.

Retaliation Punitive actions taken by employers against individuals who exercise their legal rights.

Return on investment (ROI) Calculation showing the value of expenditures for HR activities.

Rights Powers, privileges, or interests that belong to a person by law, nature, or tradition.

Right to privacy An individual's freedom from unauthorized and unreasonable intrusion into their personal affairs.

Right-to-work laws State laws that prohibit requiring employees to join unions as a condition of obtaining or continuing employment.

Rules Specific guidelines that regulate and restrict the behavior of individuals.

Safety Condition in which the physical well-being of people is protected.

Salaries Consistent payments made each period regardless of the number of hours worked.

Salting Practice in which unions hire and pay people to apply for jobs at certain companies.

Security Protection of employees and organizational facilities.

Security audit Comprehensive review of organizational security.

Selection The process of choosing individuals with the proper qualifications to fill jobs and be productive.

Selection criterion Characteristic that a person must have to do a job successfully.

Selection rate Percentage hired from a given group of candidates.

Seniority Time spend in the organization or on a particular job.

Severance pay Security benefit voluntarily offered by employers to employees who lose their jobs.

Sexual harassment Actions that are sexually directed, are unwanted, and subject the worker to adverse employment conditions or create a hostile work environment.

Situational interview Structured interview composed of questions about how applicants might handle specific job situations.

Situational judgment tests Tests that measure a person's judgment in work settings.

Statutory rights Rights based on laws or statutes.

Stock option plan Plan that gives employees the right to purchase a fixed number of shares of company stock at a specified price for a limited period of time.

Straight piece-rate system Pay system in which wages are determined by multiplying the number of units produced by the piece rate for one unit.

Strategic HR management Use of employees to gain or keep a competitive advantage, resulting in greater organizational effectiveness.

Strictness error Occurs when ratings of all employees fall at the low end of the scale.

Strike Work stoppage in which union members refuse to work in order to put pressure on an employer.

Structured interview Interview that uses a set of standardized questions asked of all job applicants.

Substance abuse Use of illicit substances or misuse controlled substances, alcohol, or other drugs.

Succession planning Process of identifying a longer-term plan for the orderly replacement of key employees.

Task Distinct, identifiable work activity composed of motions.

360-degree feedback Discusses design and use of 360° feedback and concerns with it.

Training Process whereby people acquire capabilities to perform jobs.

Turnover The process in which employees leave an organization and have to be replaced.

Undue hardship Significant difficulty or expense imposed on an employer in making an accommodation for individuals with disabilities.

Union Formal association of workers that promotes the interests of its members through collective action.

Union authorization card Card signed by an employee to designate a union as her or his collective bargaining agent.

Union security provisions Contract clauses to help the union obtain and retain members.

Utilization analysis Identifies the number of protected-class members employed in the organization and the types of jobs they hold.

Validity Extent to which a test actually measures what it says it measures.

Variable pay Compensation linked directly to individual, team, or organizational performance.

Wages Payments directly calculated on the amount of time worked.

WARN Act Identifies requirements for layoff advance notice.

Wellness programs Programs designed to maintain or improve employee health before problems arise.

Whistle-blowers Individuals who report real or perceived wrongs committed by their employers.

Work sample tests Tests that require an applicant to perform a simulated job task.

Workers' compensation Security benefits provided to persons injured on the job.

Wrongful discharge Termination of an individual's employment for reasons that are improper or illegal.

Yield ratios Comparisons of the number of applicants at one stage of the recruiting process with the number at the next stage.

Index

Note: Page numbers in *italics* refer to illustrations.

genetic bias, 43
glass ceiling, 41
globalization of business
    career development and, 76
    compensation and, 103
    management challenges and, 4
    performance incentives and, 119
    training for, *73*
    teams and, 27
graphic rating scale, 93
Great Depression, 161
grievance management, 169–71
Griggs v. Duke Power, 35
group/team incentives, 123–25

H

halo effect, 61, 97
hazard communication, 141–42
health and safety, 3, 139
    health issues and, 145–47
    injury rates/causes/costs and,
        139–40
    legal requirements and, 140–41
    OSHA and, 141–43
    safety management and, 143–45
    security concerns and, 147–48
    term clarification and, 139
health-care/medical benefits,
    131–33
health insurance, 119
Health Insurance Portability and
    Accountability Act
    (HIPAA), 128, 133
hepatitis B virus (HBV), 142
Hewlett-Packard, 87
honesty tests, 60, 153
hostile environment, 41
HR Guide—Compensation, 137
human capital, 4
human immunodeficiency virus
    (HIV), 142
human resource management. *See
    also* compensation;
    employer/employee rela-
    tions; equal employment
    opportunity (EEO); per-
    formance appraisals;
    staffing; strategic manage-
    ment; training
    activities of, 1–2
    aging workforce and, 6
    as career field, 8
    challenges of, 4–6
    defined, 1

effectiveness measures for, 2–3
ethics and, 8
global forces and, 2
importance of, 1
measuring, 15–17
nature of, 1–4
in organizations, 3–4
performance management and,
    3, 83–87, 98–99
planning and, 10–15
roles of, 6–7
human resource management
    system (HRMS), 3, 7–8, 12
human resource metrics, 15–16
    absenteeism and, 22
    importance of, 2
    turnover rates and, 23–24
    types of, 16–17
    variable pay plans and, *120*, 123
Human Resources Law Index, 156
human resource technology,
    2–3, 7–8
Huselid, Mark A., 84

I

IBM, 116
immediate confirmation, 68–69
Immigration Reform and Control
    Act (IRCA), 43, 59, 173
incentives. *See* performance
    incentives
industrial union, 159
information technology, 5, 7–8
Intel, 8
intellectual capital, 4
Internal Revenue Service (IRS),
    108, 131
International Association of Bridge,
    Structural, Ornamental
    and Reinforcing Iron
    Workers, 159
International Society for Perfor-
    mance Improvement, 99
Internet
    benefits administration and, 136
    career development and, 79
    human resource challenges
        and, 5
    recruiting from, 53–54
    sales compensation and, 123
    training on, 71
Internet resources, 18
    on benchmarking, 18
    on career planning, 82

on compensation, 118
on employee retention, 32
on equal employment, 45
on incentives, 137
on labor relations, 171
on legal information, 156
on performance
    management, 99
for recruiting, 53
on staffing, 63
on training, 82
on work/life balance, 32
interview, job, 60–61, 179–80

J

job analysis, 3, 47–50
job criteria, 86
job description, 49–50, 177–78
job design, 27
job evaluation, 84, 110
job fairs, 53
job posting, 52
job satisfaction, 20, 27
job security, 26
job sharing, 28
job-skill training, 3
job specifications, 50
Job Web, 63

K

Kirkpatrick, Donald L., 72
knowledge management, 66

L

labor law, 161–63
Labor-Management Relations Act,
    161, 162–63, 165
Labor-Management Reporting
    and Disclosure Act, 163
labor markets, 50–51, 112
Labornet, 171
labor relations/unions. *See* unions
Landrum-Griffin Act, 161, 163
living wage, 107
lockouts, 169

M

managed care, 132
management by objectives
    (MBO), 94
management development, 81–82
management rights, 166–67
market pricing, 110